Tactics of Truth: Military Principles For Waging Spiritual War

BY

ERNEST L. VERMONT

XULON PRESS

CONTENTS

PART IV. TRAINING THE FORCE

ACKNOWLEDGMENTS

This dissertation is gratefully dedicated to my longtime friend and colleague in ministry, the Rev. Theodore S. Atkinson. After suffering from stomach cancer, "Ted" joined the Church Triumphant in May of 2004. He was an inspiration to me. He provided me with encouragement, critical suggestions, and bibliographical material. He was a true warrior for the faith.

I also want to thank my former parishioner, Paul Yorkman. Paul attended my congregation at Aberdeen Proving Ground, Maryland. He regularly prayed and supported my efforts. He is a godly and wise man whose intellectual curiosity is boundless.

I want to express sincere appreciation to Dr. Charles Kraft, a professor and mentor at Fuller Theological Seminary. While taking his amazing Doctor of Ministry course, *Deep Healing and Deliverance,* I floated the idea for a dissertation. Dr. Kraft immediately saw the possibilities and encouraged me to write this work.

Lastly, I would like to thank my colleague, Chaplain (Major) Daniel Middlebrooks for his suggestion in naming this book.

ABBREVIATIONS

1SG	First Sergeant
AIT	Advanced Individual Training
AKJV	Authorized Kings' James Version of the Bible
AMC	Army Materiel Command
AMEDD	Army Medical Department
APG	Aberdeen Proving Ground, Maryland
AR	Army Regulation
BCT	Basic Combat Training
BLOS	Beyond Line of Sight
CALL	Center for Army Lessons Learned
CASEVAC	Casualty Evacuation
C2	Command and Control
C4I	Command, Control, Communications, Computer and Intelligence Systems
COA	Course of Action
CONUS	Continental United States
CI	Counter-Intelligence
CINC	Commander in Chief
CLS	Combat Life Saver
CNN	Cable News Network
CPX	Command Post Exercise
CSM	Command Sergeant Major
DA	Department of the Army
DAC	Department of the Army Civilian
DNBI	Disease and Non-Battle Injury

DS	Drill Sergeant
FLOT	Forward Line of Troops
FM	Field Manual
FTX	Field Training Exercise
G-2	Division/Corps Intelligence
HUMINT	Human Intelligence
IAAPS	Integrated Army Active Protection System
ICA	International Coalition of Apostles
IET	Individual Entry Training
INSCOM	Intelligence and Security Command
IPB	Intelligence Preparation of the Battlefield
IV	Inter-Venous
KJV	King James Version of the Bible
JACHO	Joint Administration Hospital Commission
LOS	Line of Sight
LW CAP	Living Water's Computer Assessment Program
LXX	Septuagint
METL	Mission Essential Task List
METT-T	Mission, Enemy, Terrain, Troops, Time
MI	Military Intelligence
MOS	Military Occupational Specialty
MLSA	Multi-Level Spiritual Assessment Training
OPTEMPO	Operational "Tempo"
OPD	Officers' Professional Development
NASV	New American Standard Version of the Bible
NCO	Non-Commissioned Officer
NCOPD	Non-Commissioned Officer Professional Development
NIV	New International Version of the Bible
NKJV	New King James Version of the Bible
PCUSA	Presbyterian Church United States of America
PFC	Private First Class
POI	Program of Instruction
POW	Prisoner of War
PTSD	Post Traumatic Stress Disorder
PVNTMED	Preventive Medicine
RMA	Revolution in Military Affairs

SA	Situational Awareness
S-1	Army Officer Assigned to Unit Personnel Duties
S-2	Army Officer Assigned to Unit Security and Intelligence
S-3	Army Officer Assigned to Unit Operations and Training
S-4	Army Officer Assigned to Unit Supply and Logistics
SABA	Self-Aid, Buddy-Aid
SBCCOM	Soldier Biological Chemical Command
SLSW	Strategic Level Spiritual Warfare
SME	Subject Matter Experts
SWN	Spiritual Warfare Network
TEV	Today's English Version of the Bible
TRADOC	Training and Doctrine Command
TSP	Training Support Package
WMD	Weapons of Mass Destruction
XO	Executive Officer

Prologue

Many Protestant Christians in the United States have lost their "fight" attitude. Departing from an ancient sense of ecclesiastical "militancy," too many parishioners have abrogated their place on the spiritual battlefield to cultists and other anti-Christian faith groups.

For more than five years, the United States Army has been undergoing an all-encompassing Transformation Program. This new agenda seeks to remake everything about the Army. It is aggressively planning to move from a present Legacy Force, upgrading its near-term interim force while ultimately planning for the year 2016's Objective Force.

This book will present a proposal to the Church for its own radical transformation. I believe the Church desperately needs an interim force as it seeks God's direction for an Objective Force. The centerpiece for Army transformation is the reestablishment of a new "warrior ethos." Christians must also develop a more serious and aggressive warrior ethos. While the New Testament uses military allusions, many believers in this post-modern period are not aware of Satan's strategies and tactics. Many Christians are even unaware that there is a cosmic war raging.

People who have served several years in the Army will recognize the doctrinal template placed over the book's format. I proceed consistently through a classic Army doctrinal frame of reference (lead the force, train the force, and finally, sustain the force). A soldier's education concentrates on preparation for combat. Does the Church educate its "soldiers" for combat? The Army's adage, "train as you fight," is also a useful reference. Can the Church inculcate the same approach? Lastly, the Army Rangers are known for loyalty to their battlefield wounded. They declare, "no one left behind." It is appalling how congregations treat people who suffer from emotional and spiritual wounds. Many people are left to suffer alone and in silence.

I believe the Army's doctrinal outlook can help the Church be more intentional and assertive as it conducts spiritual warfare in the twenty-first century. The Spiritual Warfare Movement is at least addressing these issues. Will the larger Church be transformed and proceed to its own Objective Force?

CHAPTER 1

INTRODUCTION

Goals of the Book

In February 2003, the United States seemed inevitably close to a second war against the forces of Saddam Hussein. In 2003, our government was placed into a "high alert" status. Every day, the media barraged our population with terror alerts and news items that heightened individual and collective stress, anxiety, and fear. The psychological and physiological effects were noticeable. As Doctors Afton Hassett and Leonard Signal of New Jersey's Robert Wood Johnson Medical School wrote recently, we're living in a "chronic heightened state of alertness and...helplessness," prompted by a "poorly defined...danger that could strike at any time in any form without warning."[1]

On September 11, 2001, the United States received a huge wakeup call. With the disintegration of the World Trade Center, the horrific Pentagon attack, and the crash of United Airlines Flight 93 in Pennsylvania, a tidal wave of shock and fear engulfed the country. The church of Jesus Christ has not been immune from society's terror trauma. Throughout the world, Christians are struggling to comfort, counsel, and comprehend.

These words are from Paul's first letter to the Corinthians: "Incredible as it sounds, we who are spiritual have the very thoughts of Christ. The spiritual man…has an insight into the meaning of everything, though his insight may baffle the man of this world."[2] (1 Corinthians 2: 18-19, JBPV) Christians possess answers and insights that can help. Believers in Christ also long for understanding. For too long many in the Church were oblivious about the world and the threat of radical Islam. Much has changed since September 11. Sensing genuine evil, many people are asking about Satanic strategy and power. Many Christians struggle to understand the strategy and tactics of the "enemy" and the dynamics of spiritual warfare.

Lester Sumrall suggested nine years ago that Christians were becoming more "militant" in their attitudes and actions: "Men think of the world as a playground. But militant Christians know otherwise. This world isn't a playground, it's a battleground. We're not here to fight, the world says, we are here to frolic. Sadly, even many Christians have adopted that attitude. Oh, they wouldn't say that in so many words, but their lifestyles and their conduct gives them away. Careless, carnal, Christianity."[3] Perhaps the Church since September 11 has really internalized what the Scriptures have said all along about our true enemy. The Apostle Paul says in Ephesians, "and pray in the Spirit on all occasions with all kinds of prayers and requests. With this in mind, be alert and always keep on praying for all the saints"[4] (Ephesians 6:18, NIV).

Christians glibly use military terms in our reference to the warfare of the Christian life. Sumrall adds, "…Yet, far too often there is little real militancy, little willingness to endure, and a noticeable lack of a conquering spirit."[5] My Army chaplain friend, Michael Coffey, makes this very point when recounting how Army Rangers practice for combat:

> Army Rangers have a proud and proven tradition of physical toughness, military skill and brains. The training is brutal; the fallout rate is high... Part of their training is hand-to-hand combat proficiency.
> The Rangers are taught simple skills that ensure the defeat of their attacker... At Fort Benning, Georgia, I would

see the Rangers practicing their combat skills everyday...
The military calls most of its training "perishable skills,"
meaning that the soldier loses the skill if he doesn't practice it. If he loses the skill, then he is far more likely to be a
casualty of the next war... Christians should learn from the
Rangers' example.[6]

The Old Testament writers liberally used warfare terms
and soldier analogies. Though the cosmic warfare motif occurs
throughout the Old Testament, it never takes center stage. This foun-
dational stage of written revelation affirms that there is a "world
in between," that there is genuine conflict within this "world," and
that this spiritual conflict affects affairs within our earthly domain.[7]
The New Testament also portrays the ministry of Jesus by using
warfare analogies and descriptions. It is crucial for us to recognize
that Jesus' view about the rule of Satan and the pervasive influence
of his army was not simply a marginal piece of first-century apoca-
lyptic thought that He happened to embrace. It is, rather, the driving
force behind everything Jesus says and does.[8] Christians today do
not hesitate to speak, pray, and preach with military terms. I believe
it is time to precisely define and clarify these terms and broaden
the discussion of the so-called "Spiritual Warfare Movement." The
United States Army has been my parish for twenty years. I have
learned some spiritual lessons through my close association with
soldiers and their families. This book will highlight these lessons.

PART 1

STRATEGIC AND TACTICAL OBJECTIVES

The Mission of the United States Army

I was recently asked why I joined the Army. At age thirty-seven, I entered active duty. I answered the questioner by first mentioning the experience of my World War II veteran father. A twenty-year-old draftee, he became a prisoner of war in 1944 during the Battle of the Bulge. There was torture, starvation, disease, and the debilitating effects of extreme cold weather. By God's grace, my father's life was spared. When I was a young boy, I distinctly remember watching with my dad the '60s television show *Combat*, starring Vic Morrow. My father and I hardly spoke during the show. And yet, I knew that he was reliving soldier experiences that both repulsed and enamored him. I learned at an early age that what Senator and former POW John McCain said about "service above self" was valuable and honorable.

Our nation and its values are indeed worth defending. In a beautiful coffee-table book entitled *The Army,* there is a chapter describing the long line of American soldiers with their 229-year history: "The Army seal bears the motto 'This We'll Defend'... To some, the motto seems obscure, but the defense of liberty is the enduring thread that connects the selfless service of an American soldier in Bosnia at the end of the twentieth century (and now again in Iraq) with similar service of a patriot who came to the defense of the revolution in 1775."[9]

I volunteered to join the Army. True, I was already an ordained clergy member of the Presbyterian Church USA (PCUSA), but somehow I felt drawn to an organization that constantly regarded "mission first." In my experience, the PCUSA as a whole has lost its sense of mission. It has become engulfed in senseless disputes and possible heresies. The PCUSA (and many other denominations) has, for almost forty years, been hopelessly languishing in malaise and a serious loss of focus. Conversely, the Army recognizes it must retool and reorient itself to perform its mission in the twenty-first century.

> From the outset, becoming a soldier meant joining a team. While the modern recruiting slogan, "Be all you can be," stressed individual fulfillment, the context of that fulfillment is the team. Soldiers become part of a unit. They learn to perform certain tasks in specified ways so that the team can achieve effects beyond the capabilities of a single individual. Teams then learn to work together so that effects of various types can be harmonized to achieve dramatic results. In essence, the history of the Army is the history of increasingly complex teams working together with continued success.[10]

With over twenty years experience as a soldier, I have learned the value of a clearly defined mission and the importance of vision statements. I will never forget the words of my commander, Colonel Fredrick E. Van Horn, when I was a new active duty chaplain at Fort Drum, New York. Colonel Van Horn said to his assembled officers out on a field exercise, "The Army exists to do only *one* thing: to wage war. Everything else is incidental." I now understand what he meant. The Army's fundamental mission has not changed. The Army must remain trained and ready in peacetime in order to deter war, deploy and commit forces rapidly to protect U.S. interests, and, if necessary, fight and win.[11]

In other large institutions, vision statements change. Institutions must change or risk irrelevancy. The Army's vision has recently undergone a dramatic transformation. Army leadership on October 12, 1999 unveiled the Army Vision, defining how it will meet the nation's requirements into the future. The Army's transformation into a force that is strategically responsive and dominant at every point on the spectrum of conflict was outlined in the Transformation Campaign Plan.[12]

This Vision Statement declares that the Army is a strategic instrument of national policy that has served our country well in peace and war for over two centuries. Soldiers enable America to fulfill its world leadership responsibilities of safeguarding our national interests, preventing global calamity, and making the world a safer place. They do this by finding peaceful solutions to the frictions between nation states, addressing the problems of human suffering, and when required, fighting and winning our Nation's wars--our non-negotiable contract with the American people.[13]

General Orders

The crucial element of any army is its soldiers. Completing a two-and-a-half-year tour in a training brigade taught me something about how the young soldier is indoctrinated. All soldiers who enlist in the United States Army must learn early in their basic training the "General Orders of the United States Army." These orders are fundamental to all a soldier does in military service.

For the US Army these orders are: (1). I will guard everything within the limits of my post, and quit my post when properly relieved. (2). I will obey my special orders and perform all my duties in a military manner. (3). I will report violations of my special orders, emergencies, or anything not covered in my instructions to the commander of my relief.[14]

To Deter Any Enemies

On December 21, 1982, I swore an oath of enlistment and became a commissioned officer in the United States Army Reserve. Brief though it was, the oath left me with one basic thought. I was now committed to be part of the armed forces. While I was officially a chaplain and a non-combatant, I knew from that moment on I could be called upon to join soldiers in a combat situation. Part of the oath says, "I will defend the Constitution against all enemies foreign or domestic."[15] To me, there was no mistaking that I was participating in an organization that would not hesitate to use force if necessary to preserve freedom.

The Cold War, of course, was won by deterring the forces of the Soviet Union and the Warsaw Pact. Today our enemies seem not to be deterred or impressed by American military might. The United States Army's White Paper entitled *Concepts for the Objective Force* succinctly describes the conceptual changes in dealing with potential enemies.

> At one end of the spectrum, creative and adaptive opponents will employ strategies to destroy U.S. resolve by attacking our homeland, killing innocent civilians, and conducting prolonged operations. Some will immerse themselves in our culture, exploit our vulnerabilities, and seek to create maximum fear... They will seek to fracture confidence in public institutions, generate economic uncertainty, and divide the focus as well as the will of the general public. Respecting the superior power of U.S. military forces, they will employ anti-access strategies... aimed at preventing or limiting U.S. impact on regional crises... Army war-gaming repeatedly demonstrates that the longer an enemy can delay effective U.S. response, the greater his chance of success.[16]

The deterrent nature of American military prowess no longer protects us. The terrorist attacks proved that the United States was not invulnerable! The American people were shocked to discover the limits of military power. Many years ago, the famous military theorist Carl von Clausewitz said, "The human mind ...has a universal thirst for clarity, and longs to feel itself part of an orderly scheme of things."[17] Perhaps one good thing came out of the surprise attacks on September 11, 2001. Americans now realize they do not know how to thwart an insidious, determined, and smart enemy. President George W. Bush can declare war on terrorism, but it is another thing to fight and win using the old rules of engagement. The great riddle of al-Qaida has been its Arab roots and its search for bases of operation in non-Arab lands. Grant the Arab rulers their due: They have exported their troubles to distant nations, driving their restless progeny in search of safe places from which the insurgents can strike at the world and, in time, settle their accounts with their own dreaded rulers.[18]

To Fight Decisively

What does it mean to "fight decisively" against such an enemy? How does one fight a foe that seems to be everywhere? Our chief enemies today are radical Islamists. Islamists do not fear our lethal capabilities enough to cease their merciless attacks.

> The enemy will resort to decentralized, small-unit operations... The enemy's goal will be to fracture U.S. and coalition resolve by degrading our capabilities and or destroying selected U.S. and allied facilities, inflicting high casualties, prolonging and increasing the cost of continued operations, and exploiting media coverage of any friendly setbacks and strikes at the U.S. homeland.[19]

This kind of warfare is called *asymmetric.* It does not resort to conventional tactics, but takes advantage of hit-and-run guerilla operations. To defeat this opponent, armies will have to think and act differently. The enemy cells must be destroyed one at a time. Since war broke out in Iraq in mid March 2003, al-Qaida and Taliban cells in Afghanistan are taking advantage of the Iraqi war diversion. There have been increased attacks on Afghan government posts. Authorities have blamed remnants of Taliban, al-Qaida, and loyalists of Gulbuddin Hekmatyar, a renegade commander labeled a terrorist by the United States. Colonel Roger King, a military spokesman, said, "There is a heightened awareness on the part of all the soldiers of potential for enemy activities based upon the initiation of hostilities in the Iraq theater."[20] Fighting decisively means being constantly vigilant against an enemy that always lies in wait and operates with surprise and deception.

To Win the Struggle

During the Persian Gulf War I was stationed in Turkey. I had the duty and privilege to travel about eighteen hundred miles per month, visiting soldiers assigned to the five hundred twenty-eighth Artillery Group. I slowly learned that Islamic culture was sophisticated and proud. Touring the "Blue Mosque" and many other places in Istanbul, I marveled at the awesome artistic and intellectual accomplishments of the Islamic world. The majority of Muslims during 1990-91 and now in 2006 actually believe that the Western powers want to eradicate their civilization from the face of the earth. Radical Islamists are convinced that the very future of Islam is at stake. For Muslims, the Persian Gulf War (1990-91) thus quickly became a war between civilizations in which the inviolability of Islam was at stake. Islamist fundamentalist groups from Egypt, Syria, Jordan, Pakistan, Malaysia, Afghanistan, Sudan, and elsewhere denounced it as a war against 'Islam and its civilization' by an alliance of 'Crusaders and Zionists.'[21] For many years, our government has been attempting to seek a just and peaceful solution to the Arab-Israeli conflict in the Middle East. There have been few successes.

Most people in the United States have little awareness of Islamic culture or its values. How can our people and our military expect to know this enemy if they do not or will not understand the root causes of the Islamists' alienation? After four hundred years, the West finally made an attempt to educate itself about Islam during the Middle Ages.

The existence of Islam was the most far-reaching problem in medieval Christendom. It was a problem at every level of experience. As a practical problem it called for action and for discrimination between the competing possibilities of Crusade, conversion, coexistence, and commercial interchange. As a theological problem it called persistently for some answer to the mystery of its existence: what was its providential role in history, was it a symptom of the world's last days or a stage in the Christian development; a heresy, a schism, or a new religion; a work of man or devil; an obscene parody of Christianity, or a system of thought that deserved to be treated with respect?... The existence of Islam made the West profoundly uneasy...The West had no access to the counsels or motives of Islam. But this incalculable factor was only an indication of a deeper incomprehension of the nature of the thing itself.[22]

Entering Fuller Seminary in 1971, I became close friends with another Master of Divinity student and his wife, who had direct ties with the Middle East and the religion of Islam. Roy and Jeanne Pope patiently shared with us their love for the Muslim world and challenged us to begin investigating the theology and culture of Islam. My provincial Christian worldview and upbringing would be forever changed. The Middle Eastern malady-victimology and the abdication of responsibility that goes with it has made its way to faraway shores. Last year, twenty-one people died in the bombing of a Tel Aviv discotheque; the nightclub explosion in Bali killed several times as many. There are no idyllic places left. The war between order and malignancy has reared its head on yet another battlefield.[23]

The United States Army must therefore fight on this new kind of battlefield. It must transform the way it thinks and conducts the fight. The Transformation Plan is a comprehensive, multi-level effort to move into the twenty-first century. The plan was already in its infancy in 1999, a full two years before the attacks of September 11, 2001. It is quite literally a revolutionary notion to rethink the business of war. Much debate and philosophical resonance in U.S. military and academic circles today focuses on whether or not we are entering, in the midst of, or departing from a revolution in military affairs (RMA).[24] A revolution in military affairs is defined as "a major change in the nature of warfare brought about by the innovative application of technologies, which combined with dramatic changes in military doctrine and operational concepts, fundamentally alters the character and conduct of operations."[25]

Army Transformation

During the American Civil War, Union and Confederate commanders were still ordering Napoleonic charges long after it should have been obvious that the tactics that won at Waterloo wouldn't work at Gettysburg. Experts also say that victors seldom learn the lessons of the previous war... The U.S. military does not want to fight the last war...

Transforming the military will affect all service members and Department of Defense civilians. New threats require new defenses, new methods, new equipment and just plain new thinking. And everyone must be involved.[26]

While I was a chaplain at Aberdeen Proving Ground (APG) from June 2000-January 2003, I had several opportunities to see exactly what the Army was doing to transform itself. Aberdeen Proving Ground is really the Army's paramount testing and evaluation installation. One day I visited the headquarters of Major General John C. Doesburg. General Doesburg was the Commander of the Soldier Biological Chemical Command (SBCCOM). As I walked through the elaborate entryway of the headquarters, I noticed a colorful display case featuring a soldier-mannequin of the futuristic "Land Warrior 1." Dressed in an odd-looking bodysuit of what appeared to be Kevlar-like armor, I marveled at the amazing technology that was being tested. That was in 2000. I see the beginnings of this "Land Warrior 1" being fielded in today's battlefields. Army Transformation is no longer a futuristic concept. It has arrived. The Army is not only committed to developing what is called "Line of Sight" (LOS) systems, but also "Beyond Line of Sight" (BLOS) computer-integrated systems. The goal is to plan aggressively for the army in the year 2016. The Army is striving for what is called complete "situational awareness." General Doesburg, briefing his officers in an Officers' Professional Development session (OPD), declared that the goals of the Army's Objective Force are fourfold. They are: to see first, understand first, act first, and finish decisively. Our Army is striving for complete "situational awareness" in which all battlefield operations are connected into an "Integrated Army Active Protection System," or IAAPS.[27]

In a speech I heard given to chaplains and chaplain assistants in a conference in Orlando, Florida, the Commander of the Army Materiel Command (AMC), four-star General Paul J. Kern reminded the attendees that there was one critical factor involved for a Fortune 500 company staying in business. Kern stated that these companies possessed a "transforming set of values that kept them alive and not their desire for profit."[28]These values for the modern U.S. Army are: responsiveness, deployability, agility, versatility, lethality, survivability and sustainability. These qualities must be "affordable and capable of reversing the conditions of human suffering rapidly and resolving conflicts decisively..."[29]

The ultimate goal of the Army Transformation Plan is the so-called Objective Force. It seeks to place a combat capable brigade anywhere in the world in ninety-six hours; put a division on the ground in one hundred twenty hours; and five divisions on the ground in theater in thirty days. To do this, the Army will gradually replace its Legacy Force with an Interim Force by 2003. Indeed, the Interim Brigade Combat Teams (ICBT) is fielded at Fort Lewis, Washington. These soldiers are being refitted with new weapon systems and new war-fighting doctrine. Moving from the Industrial Age to the Information Age, these interim units emphasize what is called, "Bioinformatics."[30] Deployed now to Iraq, the Fourth Infantry Division is the first completely digitized division.

The Army Transformation is more than an over-reliance on technology. The lowest private to the Chief of Staff of the Army is being re-educated and revitalized. The current war with Iraq has demonstrated how far this transformation is already underway.

> The Objective Force concept envisions a skilled, knowledge-based force, exploiting the revolutionary potential of information superiority and networked sensors, shooters,

supporters and decision-makers... Revised training and education that strengthen soldier and leader initiative, adaptiveness, and skills will underpin advanced material capabilities.[31]

CHAPTER TWO

The Driving Force of Jesus' Life

Recently, I viewed the Civil War movie *Gods and Generals*. In the very beginning, General "Stonewall" Jackson offers an interesting comment about war. Speaking to one of his colleagues at the Virginia Military Institute, he states, "War is the sum of all evil."[1] The connection between actual physical conflict and spiritual warfare is the element of evil itself. The ultimate goal is the same: destruction.

> The history of the world is always pictured as a swiftly running river, red with blood. It describes the men and events that cause the bloodshed; Kings and Princes, diplomats and politicians. There are wars and revolutions, insurrections and conflicts, all intruding on the territories and rights of men. But the real history is taking place on the banks, as the river rushes by, where men and women are loving each other, bearing children and nurturing them, working and building homes and trying desperately to remain untouched by the river.[2]

Jesus was aware that this bloody "river of death" affects humankind. The Apostle John proclaimed "…The Son of God appeared for this purpose, that He might destroy the works of the devil" (First

John 1: 8, NASV). The last enemy to be destroyed according to the Apostle Paul is "death" (First Corinthians 15:26, NASV). Jesus' life mission was to wage all out war against Satan and his demons, thereby bringing glory to His Father. This concept of bringing glory to God fascinated me as a young seminarian. I can still recall my first class at Fuller Seminary with Everett F. Harrison. He very calmly but forcefully summarized the whole record of Scripture by telling us that the concept of "glory" was the central recurring theme uniting Old and New Testaments. During the worship processional ushering the Ark of the Covenant into the Temple, the Old Testament chronicler utters a wonderful series of praise choruses in First Chronicles 16:28-29. To provoke more fervent worship he says, "Splendor and majesty are before him; strength and joy in his dwelling place. Ascribe to the Lord, O families of nations, ascribe to the Lord glory and strength, ascribe to the Lord the glory due his name. Bring an offering and come before him; worship the Lord in the splendor of his holiness." (NASV) In the *Bakers Dictionary of Theology*, Harrison clearly defines terms:

> The principal word in the Hebrew for this concept is *kabod,* and in the Greek *doxa,* which is derived from *dokeo,* "to think" or "to seem." These two meanings account for the two main lines of significance in classical Greek, where *doxa* means opinion (what one thinks for himself) and reputation (what others think about him), which may shade into fame or honor or praise.[3]

Throughout human history and indeed for eternity, God will be glorified. His honor and praise will be trumpeted throughout the universe. When severely criticized for allowing his disciples to praise him on Palm Sunday, Jesus pronounced that, "I tell you, if these become silent, the stones will cry out" (Luke 19: 39-40, NASV). Nothing can prevent the majesty of God from being known! Jesus' whole life demonstrated His desire to bring glory to the Heavenly Father. At the start of His ministry, Jesus emphatically stated that His Father would always glorify Himself. In His prayer coming out of the baptismal waters, Jesus said, "Father, glorify your name."

Answering responsively, the Father replied from heaven, "I have both glorified it, and will glorify it again" (John 12: 28, NASV). Jesus obeyed the Father, even to the death of the cross. He intended to be a reflection of God's glory. God indeed has a plan for the earth that helps us to realize that, despite all the earth's obvious wickedness and pain, His plan will victoriously succeed in demonstrating divine power and majesty. The spiritual goal of this high worship was to stimulate and sustain the glorification of God. There can be no higher calling on earth or heaven than to be a mouthpiece of divine praise. Satan will do absolutely anything to diminish or besmirch God's glory. There are many battles in this campaign. But the victory is already won! The Psalmist declares, "All nations whom you have made shall come and worship before you, O Lord, and they shall glorify your name" (Psalm 86: 9, NASV). The prophet Habakkuk understood that Satan would not ultimately win. Evil is doomed. Despite Israel's just punishment from the Chaldeans, the people of God are never alone. The prophet revealed in Habakkuk 2:14 an incredible glimpse of God's providential plan. This theological concept is expressed in a hymn entitled, "God is Working His Purpose Out." The lyricist Arthur Ainger, a Master at Eton wrote the words for his students. The words still put things in perspective for me.

> God is working His purpose out as year succeeds to year. God is working His purpose out and the day is dawning near. Nearer and nearer draws the time, the time that shall surely be, when the earth is filled with the glory of God as the waters cover the sea.[4]

Authentic ministry must have this end in view. Believers in Christ should be seeking to finally see God's glorious purpose overwhelm and remake the earth. The Apostle Paul says that the principal motivating force, the preeminent attitude, of the Christian soldier is this, "So whether you eat or drink or whatever you do, do it all for the glory of God" (First Corinthians 10: 31, NASV). The process of remaking the earth involves spiritual combat. Christians are on an extended deployment.

The incarnation of Jesus propelled Him into the war zone here on earth. Human combatants are enlisted in this struggle. Christ never intended to fight the war Himself. He was a soldier-recruiter *par excellence*. I know that as a soldier of Christ I have a particular place reserved for me in the line of this battle. Every follower of Christ does. In a letter that a Civil War Union officer wrote to his wife before the Battle of Bull Run, Major Sullivan Ballou speaks about his love for her and then for a greater cause. The cause "comes over me like a strong wind and bears me unresistably on with all these chains to the battlefield."[5] Just as Jesus waged war, all believers are called to their own personal spiritual battlefields. In the very familiar 1864 hymn "Onward Christian Soldiers" this theme is depicted. The boys and girls at the Sunday School in the Yorkshire wool town of Horbury Bridge were the first people to sing it. They proceeded on Whit Monday with other children from other neighboring churches. They would march along, carrying banners, with the processional cross leading the way.[6] Jesus marched, too, displaying God's glory. His entire life mission was to enter the battle line as our example and eternal champion. He was able to forcefully resist Satan's frontal attacks in the wilderness because He desired to enhance God's glory even more than life itself.

> A man must have a battle to fight, a great mission to his life that involves and yet transcends even home and family. He must have a cause to which he is devoted even unto death, for this is written into the fabric of his being...[7]

My theology of ministry focuses on a desire to experience what Moses earnestly prayed to receive. When Moses made the request of God to "show me thy glory," (Exodus 33:18, KJV) he was not speaking of the light-cloud he had already seen, but he was seeking a special manifestation of God, which would leave nothing to be desired (cf. John 14:8). Moses had a craving to come to grips with God as he was in himself. It took Moses more than eighty long years to experience a partial manifestation of God's presence.[8]

Coming to experience, and to some measure, understand God's will and ways means believers must realize they are participants

36

in a cosmic struggle. In the well-known parable of Jesus about the "talents," the servants are praised for aggressively conducting business while the master was away. Followers of Christ have already received their orders to "occupy" until he comes (Luke 19: 13, KJV). The term *occupy* is translated as "trade" or "do business." So the Church of Christ, while victorious, struggles through a spiritual guerilla war. Casualties are still occurring. The critical question is, do Christians recognize the enemy and do they understand their battlefield orders? Satanic forces are real and their mission is to attempt to destroy the Church. C.S. Lewis begins his classic *The Screwtape Letters* by describing the perpetual challenge: "There are two equal and opposite errors into which our race can fall about the devils. One is to disbelieve in their existence. The other is to believe, and to feel an excessive and unhealthy interest in them."[9]

The Mission of the Militant Church of Jesus Christ

Growing up in the Presbyterian Church during the '60s, I cannot remember a time when I was provided any theological instruction about the "militancy of the Church." The closest our congregation came to addressing the concept was our frequent singing of the great hymn "Onward Christian Soldiers." To be sure, we received instruction from the pulpit and Sunday School about the importance of evangelism and Christian service but there was little or no awareness about engaging in aggressive spiritual warfare.

Interested in what Webster's Dictionary might say about the definition of "militant," I made an Internet inquiry. Webster defines the term as from *militate*, which means "engaged in warfare; fighting; combating; serving as a soldier." Curiously, Webster adds a comment on the Church militant by saying that the earthly Christian Church is supposed to be engaged in constant warfare against its enemies and is thus distinguished from the Church Triumphant in heaven.[10] It would seem then that the Church's identity and sole reason for existence, according to Webster's Dictionary, is to engage enemies in spiritual warfare.

The theological distinction between the Church "militant" and the church "triumphant" is found in Catholic theology. There are

Roman Catholics who choose to be anonymous and name themselves "The Church Militant Forums."

This anonymous group according to their internet web site, espouses three goals: (1) to bring perspective and balance to that vast amount of information (mostly unfairly negative) about the "sex abuse" crisis in the Catholic Church; (2) to expose the organizations that are attacking the Church... (3) to provide a realistic view of the Church, how the crisis should be handled, and the victims; and (4) to pray for the Church, the faithful, and the victims, so that true Christian unity can be attained.[11]

Catholics see themselves as agents in re-establishing the "Militant Church." They define their terms in the following way:

The body of Catholic faithful in terms of spiritual warfare, is comprised of three parts: the Church Triumphant (the souls in Heaven), the Church Suffering (the souls in Purgatory), and the Church Militant (the faithful on earth). As the faithful on earth, we are engaged in constant warfare with the enemy of the Church, Satan himself.

This battle and our enemy have two dimensions, physical and spiritual. Spiritually, Satan tempts all believers to fall away from the Faith and lead us into sin. Physically, Satan uses human and physical means to attempt to undermine the Church and the Mission of Christ. The Church Militant must be involved in battle in both realms, first through the mortification of self and denial of sin, and second through the struggle against Satan trying to undermine the Church and will of Christ...

However, all must be actively engaged in struggling against those forces who would seek to destroy the Church, or more accurately, to corrupt souls and lead them to eternal damnation...[12]

Although this statement originates from the historical context of sexually abusive priests, it is an accurate summary of what many Christians basically believe about the ultimate mission of the Church. We are to engage Satan on all fronts. The question is how do we do that in the twenty-first century?

The Necessity of Spiritual War

Warfare actions either in the physical or heavenly realm, start with a threat analysis. Who or what is the threat? If Satan and his demonic hordes are the instigators of physical and spiritual destruction, how or why should they be defeated? While many Christians today tacitly agree that the Bible teaches about wickedness and social evils, the belief in a person named "Satan" for modern society is indeed a stretch.

> Nothing commends Satan to the modern mind. It is bad enough that Satan is spirit, when our worldview has banned spirit from discourse and belief. But worse, he is evil, and our culture resolutely refuses to believe in the real existence of evil, preferring to regard it as a kind of systems breakdown that can be fixed with enough tinkering. Worse yet, Satan is not a very good intellectual idea. Once theology lost its character as reflection on the experience of *knowing* God, and became a second-level exercise in *knowing about,* the experiential ground of theology began to erode away.[13]

Satan is regarded by many persons as not the personification of evil but merely, as Morton Kelsey writes, as "intellectually indefensible...a representation of peoples' experience..."[14] If Morton Kelsey is correct, why should the Church bother to fight him? Walter Wink argues that we need a "resymbolization" of evil. Without a means of symbolization, however, evil cannot come to conscious awareness and thus be consciously resisted. Like an undiagnosed disease, it rages through society, and we are helpless to produce a cure.[15]

I believe Walter Wink is very wrong about his conception of Satan. He insists that society merely needs a new way of conceptualizing evil. My reading of Scripture and experience has taught me that Satan has a distinct personality. He thwarts people from coming to know and receive the gospel, and he assaults the name of Jesus. I know Satan can be resisted because I have done so.

During my first pastorate in Southeast Alaska, I encountered Satanic power in a young Native-American woman in the Tlingit village of Hoonah. My friend and colleague, Reverend Joseph Bettridge, and I were fervently trying to provide pastoral counseling to his parishioner. There had been violent assaults between her and her husband. Whenever they were together, physical and verbal abuse would begin. They could not remain in the same house. I remember that we discovered a common denominator: the woman's hand-woven shawl. The garment was a present from her Navajo father. The woman's father was known to be a powerful shaman in New Mexico. The woman had been directed by her father to always wear the garment for protection. When her husband became a Christian, the violence began between them.

One day Bettridge and I attempted to pray for this couple and felt the shawl needed to be destroyed. We attempted to burn it with the husband's permission. Initially, it would not burn! After much prayer, the garment burned and the violence stopped. Throughout my thirty-two years of ministry, I have encountered much more than what Wink calls a "two-dimensional bogeyman."

The Weapons in the Arsenal

When clergy enter military service, they receive instruction in the provisions of the Geneva Convention. Chaplains are told that they are non-combatants. As such, they may not be compelled to carry or use weapons of any kind. I do remember that while I was at chaplain officer basic training in 1983, my chaplain colleagues and I did receive what the Army calls "familiarization training." We briefly fired rifles, threw hand grenades, and learned some basic self-protection measures. Familiarization is, of course, a far cry from weapon proficiency. I believe that Christians have exactly this problem. They are vaguely familiar with spiritual weaponry, but not at all adept in their capabilities and usage. Soldiers need to know about their basic weapon systems and receive regular re-qualification training. Many Christians have read what Scripture says about spiritual weapons, but have only theoretical knowledge and training in spiritual weaponry.

> Paul (the Apostle) enumerated seven spiritual weapons. Five of these are objective endowments from God (truth, righteousness, the gospel, salvation and the Spirit/the word of God) and two stress our responsibility (faith and prayer). Our responsibility is also implicit in the five gifts from God. While this list of spiritual resources ("weapons") does not exhaust all divine bestowments available to Christians, it represents the essence of all that is vital to waging successful warfare against the powers of darkness. The nature of spiritual warfare, as Paul portrayed it here, is primarily concerned with Christian conduct and spreading the gospel—not with exorcism or eradicating structural evil. The heart of spiritual warfare could best be summarized as resistance and proclamation.[16]

Conducting Spiritual Warfare in a Postmodern World

When military commanders prepare to wage war, they must know everything they can about the enemy and their battlefield environment. The real goal is to get into the decision-making cycle or the mindset of an adversary so that he can be defeated. Spiritual warfare in the twenty-first century is conducted on various battlefields of the so-called "postmodern world."

The mindset of this world is very different from the "modern" world. Modernism stressed a great faith in science and technology and therefore elevated rationalism. Things needed to make sense. My wife and I, who are "baby boomers" and immersed in a "make sense" world-view, comment to each other that we feel "out of touch" with the attitudes and mores of this present culture. Television programming especially seems intentionally focused on our twenty-five-year-old daughter's generation. It is a generation that seems to place more value on feeling and experience and less on rationality.

Before leaving my position as the training Brigade Chaplain at APG, I had a wonderful and enlightening opportunity to instruct drill sergeants about the so-called "Bridger Generation." Our soldiers were all members of this generation. The Drill Sergeants were all from a previous generation. The Bridger Generation was from 1977-1994 and, according to the 1995 United States Census, numbers seventy-two million people. It will be the dominant adult population for at least one-half of the twenty first century. The "Bridgers" will not fit the mold or expectations of the baby boomers.[17] If, as a seminary professor once old me, "the Church is only one generation away from extinction," we must learn to communicate the Gospel to this generation before we lose the opportunity. The post-modern culture must be understood and bridged. Strategic and tactical methods must be devised in order to conquer Satanic attempts to deceive countless millions. Spiritual intelligence needs to be accumulated to do precisely what Clinton Arnold proposes. That is, to "resist and proclaim."

> Since Post Modernism is relatively new (and a fashionable 'bandwagon') theory, it is actually quite difficult to pin point its basic characteristics, it means many different things to different thinkers and it is constantly being updated anyway... [Post Modernism]...is the belief that direction, evolution and progression have ended in social history, and society is based instead upon the decline of absolute truths, and the rise of relativity...[18]

The "decline of absolute truths and the rise of relativity" is not an especially new idea. In fact, many of the philosophical and theological tenets of postmodernism are merely re-workings of notions that have challenged people of faith for many centuries. Solomon reminds us in Ecclesiastes: "The thing that hath been, it is that which shall be; and that which is done is that which shall be done: and there is no new thing under the sun" (Ecclesiastes 1: 9, AKJV).

Postmodernism then is not a new enemy for the Church. It purports to be non-exclusive and strives to allow all truth to be equally relevant and important. The basic notions of postmodernism are these: The decline of any absolute truths—the creation of relativity, the lack of purpose and direction in historical change (decline of teleology), the fragmentation and division of all academic subjects into a variety of perspectives—with no "answers," no agreement; the fragmentation of cultural forms into a "playful celebration" of chaos.[19] The notion that society can and indeed should strive for a "playful celebration of chaos" is exactly what the enemy of our souls desires to replicate in our minds. Satan delights in causing humanity to think that our freewill, relativistic "choices" are quite natural and that this spiritual evolution from God's absolute truth is, in fact, something that should be cultivated and honored. C.S. Lewis' Uncle Screwtape relays this tidbit of Satanic "wisdom" to his charge, Wormwood: "We know that we have introduced a change of direction in his (i.e. Man's) course which is already carrying him out of his orbit around the Enemy; but he must be made to imagine that all the choices which have effected this change of course are trivial and revocable. He must not be allowed to suspect that he is now, however slowly, heading right away from the sun on a line which will carry him into the cold and dark of utmost space."[20]

The Church struggles against a real and formidable adversary, who contends on various battlefields. Satan primarily tries to overcome the Church of Jesus Christ. He is accomplished in subverting cultures, governments, marriages, families, and any other human institution. His ultimate goals are to deceive, divide, and destroy. When one specifically addresses the philosophical constructs of postmodernism, it is important to understand its scope. When applied to society, a postmodern world would be one where there is no universally agreed upon principle of knowledge and organization. Six basic principles include: (1) The growth of the service sector; (2) The spread of globalization; (3) Fragmentation; (4) Massive loss of faith in science; (5) The end of meta-narratives; and (6) An abandonment of the optimism of the Enlightenment.[21]

The so-called "end of the meta-narrative" in many Western cultures has particular relevance to spiritual warfare theology. If the grand human stories are irrelevant or worse—non-existent—what is left to tie human societies together? It would seem that Satan has indeed unleashed a disease upon postmodernism that he originally wished to show in the Garden of Eden—namely, the illusion of humanity's knowledge and power relative to God's.

A relatively new strand of theorists believes our re-definition of experience is moving us into a post-modern condition which the overarching principles on which society is based, meta-narratives, are broken down. Arthur C. Clarke's unprecedented novel, *The City and the Stars*, was published in 1954, twenty years before the articulation of post-modern theory... Though Clarke adheres to and illustrates our move to the post-modern condition, he resists a full transition to post-modernity by his belief in the power of the human spirit to act as a new meta-narrative for society.[22]

If there is no absolute truth and relativity reigns supreme, then the resulting ethical and spiritual fragmentation will certainly tighten its demonic grip over the Church and society. The prophet Isaiah's words come to mind. Bible commentators believe Isaiah 59 is a "community lament." The lament is for Israel.[23] Maybe it is for us as well. "So justice is far from us, and righteousness does not reach us. We look for light, but all is darkness; for brightness, but we walk in deep shadows. Like the blind we grope along the wall, feeling our way like men without eyes. At midday we stumble as if it were twilight; among the strong, we are like the dead...So justice is driven back, and righteousness stands at a distance; truth has stumbled in the streets, honesty cannot enter. Truth is nowhere to be found, and whoever shuns evil becomes a prey" (Isaiah 59: 9-10; 14-15, NIV).

Reminiscent of the Apostle Paul's description of the believer's "armor," Isaiah delineates the body armor of God Himself. "He (God) saw that there was no one, he was appalled that there was no one to intervene; so his own arm worked salvation for him, and his own righteousness sustained him. He put on righteousness as his breastplate, and the helmet of salvation on his head; he put on the garments of vengeance and wrapped himself in zeal as his cloak. According to what they have done, so will he repay wrath to his enemies and retribution to his foes..." (Isaiah 59: 16-18, NIV).

The Old Testament's Joshua is a type of the warrior-leadership Jesus personified. The Promised Land is always won with a tremendous fight. Leaders must be willing to be flexible and exercise battlefield savvy. The tactics of warfare constantly change because enemies repeatedly adapt their methods and weapons. The institutional Church and individual Christians must be willing to change warfare methods, training, and treating their wounded.

There are no formulas with God. Period. So there are no formulas for the man who follows him. God is a Person, not a doctrine. He operates not like a system—not even a theological system, but with all the originality of a truly free and alive person. 'The realm of God is dangerous,' says Archbishop Anthony Bloom. 'You must enter into it and not just seek information about it.' Take Joshua and the Battle of Jericho. The Israelites are staged to make their first military strike into the Promised Land and there's a lot hanging on this moment, the morale of the troops, their confidence in Joshua, not to mention their reputation that will precede them to every other enemy that awaits. This is their D-Day, so to speak, and word is going to get around. How does God get the whole thing off to a good start? He has them march around the city blowing trumpets for a week; on the seventh-day, he has them do it seven times and then give a big holler. It works marvelously, of course. And you know what? It never happens again. Israel never uses that tactic again[24]

In this postmodern era, the Church should imitate the Army. The United States Army values adaptability and constantly reevaluates its strategy and tactics. As previously indicated, the Army has been rapidly moving towards a significant transformation since 1999. Will the Church of Jesus Christ also be able to conquer the tactics of post-modernism? In a report presented to the European Strategy Group, Ross P. Rohde using research performed in Spain summarizes the situation: "The way the modern Church responds to this new philosophical tidal wave will determine whether we reap a new and exciting harvest or whether postmodern society will set us aside as irrelevant."[25]

The issue then is how to most effectively minister to postmodernists. In the final analysis, it involves a war with Satan and his divisive and destructive ideas and tactics. In order to secure victory, believers must undergo a paradigm shift. They must not be afraid to confront change while holding fast to orthodoxy.

In my own denomination, the Presbyterian Church USA, congregants are somewhat aware of this cultural change but it is the hierarchy of the Church that seems theologically confused and hopelessly out of touch with the majority of congregants. In a renewal publication for Presbyterians, Karl Barth's biographer and former assistant, Eberhard Busch, expresses Barth's heart. "Barth is often quoted, 'You have to read the Bible and the newspaper in order to be a good minister in the church...your ear and your heart must be fully in the Scripture, and, on the other side, you must understand the thinking of the people to see what is needed."[26]

Growing up in an evangelical Presbyterian congregation, I distinctly remember my home pastor relentlessly reminding his parishioners about Biblical authority. Do we really believe in both objective and exclusive truth? Are we absolutely committed to the theological maxim that the Bible is "the only rule of faith and practice?"[27] The fundamental issue then is what is our source of truth? Are these truths absolute and trustworthy? How do we communicate absolute truths to a society in transition that rejects absolute truth? For many, it is the seminaries that need a complete theological overhaul. The concept of heresy seems not only politically incorrect, but also thoroughly out of date.

> It seems worth noting that the liberated seminary at its zenith has finally achieved a condition that has never before prevailed in Christian history: Heresy simply does not exist. Christian doctrine and catechesis, after long centuries of struggle against heresy, have finally found a way of overcoming heterodoxy altogether, by banishing it as a concept legitimately teachable within the hallowed walls of the inclusive multicultural, doctrinally experimental institution.[28]

Modernists cannot tolerate doctrinal fuzziness. As Rohde reminds us, "Doctrines are our (modernists') theological facts. (Modernists)…have a tendency to disagree and even argue over these facts because to get the facts right is of very high value to modernists. (They) have a low tolerance for ambiguity in doctrine because the modern mind wants everything clearly explained."[29] Postmodernists, on the other hand, seem to thrive on ambiguity and inclusivism. Tolerance is the watchword.

In any war, getting the facts right is the function of the intelligence services. Armies everywhere know the critical value of collecting, processing, and analyzing what are called "raw" intelligence sources. People of faith also have an obligation to be "wise as serpents" (Matthew 10:16, NKJV). There was no place for ambiguous or misleading information during the surveillance of Jerusalem's broken walls. The Biblical text Nehemiah 1: 11-13 sets forth Nehemiah's desire for absolute clarity about his surroundings. He tells us about the process of obtaining actionable intelligence when surveying the crumbled walls of Jerusalem. "I went to Jerusalem, and after staying there three days, I set out during the night with a few men. I had not told anyone what my God had put in my heart to do for Jerusalem…By night I went out through the Valley Gate toward the Jackal Well and the Dung Gate, examining the walls of Jerusalem, which had been broken down, and its gates, which had been destroyed by fire." (NIV) The translation of this term *examine* in the NIV is instructive. The Aramaean means "to look on something," the Arabic means "to investigate," and the Hebrew means "to look on, to consider, to direct the eyes and thoughts to some object."[30] The root of the Hebrew word is "to circuit" or "to go round about," as if moving around a certain environ.[31] In order for Nehemiah to battle the obstructionism of Sanballat, Tobiah, and Geshem, Nehemiah had to conceal and bypass his critics. In truth, Nehemiah was a silent intelligence warrior. The Church needs more actionable intelligence to defeat the demonic soldiers of Satan. The United States Army values its intelligence services now more than ever.

PART II. INTELLIGENCE PREPARATION

CHAPTER THREE

The Necessity of Military Intelligence:
Knowing the Enemy

On July 1, 2003, I was reassigned to a military intelligence unit in Fort Meade, Maryland. I soon realized I had entered a strange new world. This organization was a counter-intelligence unit. In order to work among these dedicated and highly trained soldiers and civilians, I was required to obtain a top-secret clearance. Shortly after my arrival, I was asked to provide an invocation at a change of command ceremony. Printed on the program was the Military Intelligence Soldier's Creed. It reads:

> I am a soldier first, but an intelligence professional second to none. With pride in my heritage, but focused on the future, Performing the first task of an army: to find, to know and never lose the enemy. With a sense of urgency and tenacity, professional and physical fitness, and above all, integrity, for in truth lies victory. Always at silent war while ready for a shooting war; the silent warrior of the army team.[1]

Collecting Information and the Intelligence Estimate

Here is the principal issue for any military organization—namely, to know the enemy. To know the enemy requires a tremendous surveillance, analysis, and counterintelligence effort. For a commander to effectively lead troops into battle, he or she must first request an "intelligence estimate." Napoleon Bonaparte once commented, "If I always appear prepared, it is because before entering on an undertaking, I have meditated long and foreseen what may occur."[2] This intelligence is constantly being refined and updated to meet the changing battlefield situation. Often called the "fog of war," the military expects many unforeseen circumstances and that any enemy will adapt and do the unexpected. Psychological profiles of enemy commanders and known enemy responses to past battle scenarios are all factored into fighting real or potential combatants. Elaborate on-the-ground war-gaming exercises and simulations are held regularly in various parts of the world. One exercise is called the Basic Combat Training Program. This program is all computer-driven but involves people who often are "cross-trained" in areas in which they have limited expertise. The purpose of course is to train warriors that, when confronted by casualties and other battlefield exigencies are able to assume staff functions that are ordinarily foreign to them. But fundamental to all army operations is the construction of the intelligence estimate. The process is called the Intelligence Preparation of the Battlefield (IPB).

The Intelligence Preparation of the Battlefield

IPB is a systematic, continuous process of analyzing the threat and environment in a specific geographic area. It is designed to support staff estimates and military decision-making. Applying the IPB process helps the commander selectively apply and maximize his combat power at critical points in time and space on the battlefield by: (1) Determining the threat's likely Course of Action or COA and (2) Describing the environment a unit is operating within and the effects of the environment on that unit.[3]

The collection of intelligence data is a very precise and sometimes tedious process. Staff officers pay particular attention to the environment of the battlefield and the enemy's "relative combat power." Small bits of information taken separately seem to mean nothing. However, when other data is added to the puzzle, a complete picture becomes clear. The timely and accurate collection, processing and dissemination of the intelligence product may mean the difference between life and death for soldiers in the field.

Army commanders need to know enemy capabilities, tactics, equipment, and even the personalities of their opponents. One of the means of collecting intelligence involves soldier teams that engage in meticulous scouting. Presently, the Army employs both long (LRS) and short-range surveillance. In a recent *Army Times* article describing the Army's long-range surveillance training course, the importance of this mission becomes evident: "Like the long-range reconnaissance patrols common during the Vietnam War, soldiers in these specialized units operate in six-man teams deep behind enemy lines with little or no support for their five-to-seven-day missions."[4] Detailing the specifics of this Fort Benning, Georgia, course, the article further states, "In addition to covering terrain, enemy situation and communications, students map out the easily-forgettable details such as how rally points will be selected and how they plan to cross danger areas."[5] While LRS units operate individually and dismounted, scout units are usually in vehicles and provide commanders short-range reconnaissance. The debate in the Army is whether to require scouts to be trained at the school originally created for their long-range counterparts.[6] The bottom line is, whether gaining intelligence information from either short or long-range surveillance units, commanders in the field need a twenty-four-hour, all-terrain asset. Very special soldiers are selected to provide this reconnaissance.

The IPB then includes a four-step process. The process is repeated each time in sequence. The steps are: (1) Define the battlefield environment; (2) Describe the battlefield's effects; (3) Evaluate the threat; and (4) Determine threat COA's. IPB is conducted prior to and during the commander's initial planning for an operation, but is also performed during the conduct of the operation.[7]

The first step then is to define the battlefield environment. The intent is to develop a product that gives the commander an overview of the "battle-space." That is, what are the boundaries or areas of interest (AI) in which the battle will be fought? Obviously what affects enemy forces will certainly affect friendly forces. When the AI is established, gaps in current intelligence holdings are identified. Army Field Manual 34-130 continues:

> To focus the remainder of the IPB process, the G2/S2 identities characteristics of the battlefield which require in-depth evaluation of their effects on friendly and threat operations... The G2/S2 establishes the limits of the AI to focus analytical and intelligence collection efforts on the geographic areas of significance to the command's mission... Once approved by the commander, the specific intelligence required to fill gaps in the command's knowledge of the battlefield environment and threat situation becomes the command's initial intelligence requirements.[8]

The second step in the IPB seeks to evaluate in depth the limitations and opportunities that the environment affords to both friendly and threat forces. There is particular care given to describing an area's infrastructure, such as politics, civilian press, local population, city systems, and facilities.[9] Battles are never fought without an understanding of the conflict's unique context.

The third step in the IPB earnestly evaluates the threat—that is, enemy forces.

> The G2/S2 and his staff analyze the command's intelligence holdings to determine how the threat *normally* (Italics mine) organizes for combat and conducts operations under similar circumstances... When operating against a new or less well-known threat, he may need to develop his intelligence data- bases and threat models concurrently.[10]

Notice that the field manual uses the term *normally* when referring to how an enemy is expected to fight. One of the problems

Coalition and American forces are having with the current threat in Iraq is the enemy's increasing sophistication and professional tactics.

What about domestic terrorism? The Army must be flexible in developing new threat models for a conventional war because our enemy today is conducting a so-called "asymmetric war" success-fully on our own shores. The urgent need of developing better intelli-gence (i.e. for emerging threats) was raised during the Congressional confirmation hearings of General Richard Myers as Chairman of the Joint Chiefs of Staff just fifty-two hours after the September 11 attacks.

> For months, Pentagon officials have said they have ambitious plans for updating intelligence operations... Lawmakers agreed with senior military leaders that more must be done to modernize the ways the government gathers intelligence...[11]

The last step in the IPB process is evaluating the threat.

> Given what the threat normally prefers to do, and the effects of the specific environment in which he is operating now, what are his likely objectives and the COAs available to him?[12]

While the basic process is still relevant, the war on terrorism is forcing America's and other nations' armies to upgrade their information warfare technologies. At the same time, it is woefully apparent that our nation's human intelligence (HUMIT) needs to be increased and better utilized. There is no substitute for human intel-ligence data collection.

As Christians, we must internalize what Holy Scripture tells us about the real battlefield. "Our struggle is not against flesh and blood, but against the rulers, against the powers, against the world forces of this darkness, against the spiritual forces of wickedness in the heavenly places" (Ephesians 6:12, NASV). How then shall we conceive and respond to preparing an intelligence estimate of

Satan and his forces? What are his emerging threats? Several years ago while considering the war on terrorism, I suddenly thought that Satan was the ultimate terrorist! He lies in wait to maim and eventually destroy all that crosses his path. He revels in the shadows and does not usually desire to pursue frontal attacks against the church. Satan prefers to drain a believer's effectiveness by making that person spiritually weak and indifferent to the real war: the invisible one.

Satan and His Army: The Ultimate Terrorists

While attending a Doctor of Ministry course in November 1999 entitled "Deep Healing and Deliverance" with Charles Kraft, I witnessed the deceptive and mercilessness nature of demonic activity. In a post-seminar paper, I wrote the following summary of the class activities:

During the various ministry sessions held in conjunction with Dr. Kraft's class, I remember him saying to us that "Satan is a master of bluff." Numerous classmates during their ministry times had unbeknownst to them a "familial or ancestral" spirit or another demon, which had attached itself to the person's emotional, physical or spiritual life. I recorded each day my reflections on these ministry sessions.

The following entry is from November 10, 1999:

Today's session was very draining emotionally and also exhilarating. After a brief teaching period, Dr. Kraft conducted our first ministry time. A Christian brother named "J" had as he said, "submitted his personal inventory first and thus, was seated in the chair of blessing." After a relatively brief period dealing with inner child emotions and some historical explanations, Dr. Kraft confronted several demons and commanded them in Jesus' name to come to attention and reveal themselves. There was fairly strong resistance from spirits named "Shame," "Death," "Destroyer," and

"Lust." It soon became apparent from their respective voices that each was tied to stronger and more insidious demons... Soon Kraft challenged generational spirits to reveal themselves. After considerable reluctance, voices manifested themselves. There was a lot of grimacing, hissing, mocking laughter, sighing and other verbal and non-verbal signs that other personalities were indeed present. Another class member passed several notes. I wrote three notes and passed them along... I sensed a spirit of slavery, murder and then incest or the fear of incest. Dr. Kraft used the first two "words of knowledge" and the spirits were called out...

In my notes from 11 November, 1999, I wrote:

The time spent with "T" proved to be the most amazing and intriguing session to date. Dr. Kraft also told the other class members that he had suspected that "T" had Multiple Personality Disorder or as it is called now, Dissociative Identity Disorder. No one in the class had ever seen what followed. Not only did Kraft deal with separate demons but also with six alternate personalities AND their individual demons. In effect, this session would free "T" from numerous demons but also integrate her alters back into her core personality.[13]

The Nature of Satan's Strategy and Tactics

Like most terrorists, Satan lies in wait. He continually looks for human vulnerabilities or what the Army calls a "soft target." An army's first task is indeed "to find, to know, and never to lose the enemy." Human beings live their lives in enemy territory. Secondly, as Satan possesses a delegated authority from God, he is not in control of anything. Thirdly, Jesus was the greatest obstacle in Satan's scheme. Fourthly, thwarted in his ultimate aim, Satan seeks to ruin as much of God's creation as possible. Fifthly, Satan is sterile and cannot create anything from nothing. Sixthly, Satan has a lot of authority and power. Lastly, Satan's kingdom is well organized.[14]

If we were to apply the Army's methodology in preparing an intelligence estimate of the Church's spiritual war, what would it look like? The Bible reveals much about Satan and his army of demons. For example, we are taught that Satan is "the father of lies." (John 8:44, NIV) In Matthew's Gospel, we read Jesus' words: "From the days of John the Baptist until now the kingdom of heaven suffers violence, and violent men take it by force." (Matthew 11: 12, NASV) God-directed people will endure physical and spiritual attacks in their lives. The context of this Scripture focuses on the true identity of John the Baptist. Later, in verse 18, many people said of John, "he has a demon." Satan thrives on confusion and deception. At any cost, he maneuvers people into believing falsehoods and is able to blind people to the truths of God. Early in Jesus' ministry, the Jewish religious leaders viciously accused Jesus of casting out demons because He was "Beelzebub, the ruler of the demons." (Luke 11: 15, NASV) These religious leaders were totally incapable of perceiving spiritual truth. Satan himself had blinded their spiritual eyes. Paul commented on this phenomenon in 2 Corinthians 4: 3-4.

The central question in any intelligence estimate is: who is the enemy and what are his capabilities and intent? Within the Christian community and our society in general, there is considerable debate as to the origin, identity, and purpose of Satan. One popular view comes from a professor of religion at Princeton University named Elaine Pagels. In her book, *The Origin of Satan,* she clearly expresses her philosophical bias. She states her interest as "the social implications of the figure of Satan: how he is invoked to express human conflict and to characterize human enemies within our own religious traditions."[15] Pagels views the Gospel of Mark's emphasis on Satan's assault on Jesus by explaining her understanding of the Biblical account in light of extra-biblical Jewish writings.

Mark deviates from mainstream Jewish tradition by introducing "the devil" into the crucial opening scene of the gospel, and goes on to characterize Jesus' ministry as involving continual struggle between God's spirit and the demons, who belong, apparently to Satan's "kingdom" (see Mark 3: 23-27).[16]

Pagels reveals in her book's thesis a thinly veiled disdain for the biblical record. Her use of the word *apparently,* when referring to Satan's kingdom, indicates her theological bias. She further outlines her sociological perspective by stating that her "...research, then, reveals certain fault lines in Christian tradition that have allowed for the demonizing of others throughout Christian history... I invite you to consider Satan as a reflection of how we perceive ourselves and those we call 'others'."[17]

The clear reading of Scripture reveals that Satan is no mere psychological "reflection" but a real and intensely personal enemy to all who trust in Jesus. There is a twofold perspective in Scripture that presents both a so-called "Godward and Satanward" view. James Kallas, in his book *Jesus and the Power of Satan*, clearly describes the difference.

> There is this element of tragedy which stalks man in God's own world, and neither the goodness of the world nor its demonic nature can be lost sight of. The raw material is there, as the Godward and Satanward views lie side-by-side, contradictory, yet both present in the teaching of Jesus. He had the courage to say two opposite and opposed things. Paul had that same courage—courage to be comprehensive even if not consistent. The later church of our day is less courageous, opting for only half the truth—and thus in danger of losing all truth.[18]

In lesson two of Kraft's MG714 Doctor of Ministry course, he outlines three very crucial dimensions or as he says, "encounters" that are vital to the experience and communication of the Gospel. They are: (1) allegiance leading to relationship (2) truth leading to understanding, and (3) spiritual power leading to freedom.[19] Kraft believes that Satan attacks all three of these dimensions, attempting to usurp or kill any possibility of the "God-connected" life. To understand this strategy means that believers, particularly those in church leadership, can short-circuit satanic devices. For Kraft, though, it is the "freedom" dimension that can only be realized through a power encounter. He states: "Satanic power must be defeated with

God's power. It cannot be defeated simply with truth or a correct allegiance, though these help." Under this dimension, the Church is experienced as both a hospital where wounds are healed and an army that attacks the enemy, defeating him at both the ground level and the cosmic level.[20]

Taking and Holding the Enemy's Ground

A soldier cannot take and hold an enemy's ground unless he employs more combat power than his opponent. It usually takes what the Army affectionately calls "boots on the ground"—that is, foot soldiers to take and hold an enemy's terrain. The Church needs more knowledgeable soldiers and troops on the battlefield. In the spiritual realm, there are two battlegrounds: the "world" of men and the "kingdom of God." Sooner or later, these two clash, and the fundamental question becomes who is in charge? Who has the real authority to rule and overrule? How is it possible for God's power to permeate the world of men? A man who surely knew all about authority and power was the German pastor, Dietrich Bonhoeffer. In 1931, eight years before Hitler invaded Poland and started World War II, he declared:

> No man can look with undivided vision at God and at the world of reality so long as God and the world are torn asunder. Try as he may, he can only let his eyes wander distractedly from one to the other. But there is a place at which God and the cosmic reality are reconciled, a place at which God and man have become one. That and that alone is what enables man to set his eyes upon God and the world at the same time...[21]

As Bonhoeffer faced the satanic forces of a burgeoning Nazism, we in the twenty-first century also face other manifestations of evil. In his first work, *Sanctorum Communio,* he reminds us that a person comes into existence only when, "he is passionately involved in a moral struggle, and confronted by a claim which overwhelms him."[22] Individual Christians can dare to wield the authority of Jesus' name.

During the Reformation, men like Luther, Calvin, and others certainly believed they were confronting tremendous arrogance and evil that permeated the entire society. The reformers emphasized their formidable verbal skills promoting solid biblical teaching and preaching. They hoped they would in time transform the world dominated by demonic institutions and structural evil. This cognitive approach largely ignored the experiential dimensions of the faith.[23] In Charles Kraft's view, the Church discounted not only the experiential dimension of the faith but also "power encounters" so prevalent in the Gospels. Kraft states that, "Jesus called the twelve to *be with him*" (Kraft's italics) and only then to communicate and engage in power ministry (Mark 3:14). [24]Kraft argues that the evangelical community is essentially afraid of exercising the power that Jesus bestowed upon the Church at Pentecost. The Church he says has capitulated in favor of a mode of operation that over-emphasizes a rationalistic world-view at the expense of a more relational approach that provides people freedom from Satan's bondage. What remains is a Church that is largely uninformed and extremely frightened by head-on power encounters with demons.[25] In support of his point Kraft corrects the English translation of John 8:32. "If we are true to the original Greek (and the Hebrew worldview behind it), John 8:32 should be translated: 'You will *experience* the truth and the truth will set you free'."[26]

Following the doctrine of the Army's IPB, the next step is to describe the battlefield's effects. Clearly, one of the effects is that spiritual warfare creates a great deal of apprehension and demands much physical, mental, and spiritual effort. The Bible portrays people of faith as being in a life situation that requires they escape and evade the "roaring lion" (I Peter 5:8, RSV). The Apostle Paul, while a prisoner in Rome, writes his beloved letter to the Philippians and tells them to "work out their salvation with fear and trembling." (Philippians 2: 12, NASV) Further, he takes great pains to paint an ominous picture of this world that believers must never forget. "Do all things without grumbling or disputing; that you may prove yourselves blameless and innocent, children of God above reproach in the midst of a crooked and perverse generation, among whom you appear as lights in the world" (Philippians 2: 14-15, NASV). Paul is saying that Christians must be constantly on guard against influences that will tarnish reputations and inflict all kinds of physical, emotional, and spiritual wounds upon individual believers and the Church as a whole! In effect, Paul sets the conditions for the need of periodic spiritual cleansing and deliverance. In the New Testament, the story of Jesus is told against the backdrop of the demonic. One of the important motifs running through the story is conflict— and not just conflict between Jesus and human opponents. All of the Evangelists portray Jesus as being in conflict with Satan and demons.[27]

According to Sydney Page, during inter-testamental times, the Jews grieved over their intense suffering and captivity. This provided the ideal environment for collective spiritual introspection involving the likely assault from malevolent spiritual forces.[28] The point is God's people have always known about the existence and interference of Satan and demons. What are demons? Soldiers of the cross should borrow from the MI soldiers' creed. They must "find, know, and never lose the enemy."

> The Gospels and Acts, especially the synoptic Gospels, make frequent reference to the powers that are in league with Satan. They are most often designated as "demons," which normally translates the diminutive *daimonion*. There are over fifty occurrences of *daimonion* with the meaning "demon" in the Gospels and Acts, compared to nine references in the rest of the New Testament. The noun *daimon*, also rendered "demon," occurs only in Matthew 8:31. Another expression with the same meaning is "unclean spirit" (*akatharton pneuma*), which appears twenty-one times half of which are in Mark.[29]

My first lessons about demonology came from the late Derek Prince. I will never forget Prince categorically stating that Christians *can* have a demon. He made the distinction between being demon-possessed and being demonized. Many who are involved in deliverance ministry today object to the term *demon-possessed,* arguing that it should be replaced by the word *demonized* because "possessed" suggests that the victim is completely under the control of a demon.[30]

When Jesus first encounters a demon, it is in the synagogue among religious people in Capernaum. In Mark 1: 23f, a man "with an unclean spirit" (NASV) pitifully cries out to Jesus. The demon asks various questions that reveal much about demons' knowledge and power. It is apparent that the answers to these provocative questions will provide important clues in our spiritual intelligence estimate. Asking rhetorically, "What do we have to do with you?" the demon challenges Jesus to a power encounter. It is also important to understand that, as Page puts it, "a fundamental conflict between those of his ilk and Jesus" ensues.[31]

Because there is a cosmic and earthly spiritual conflict, it is imperative for soldiers of Christ to carefully evaluate the threat. The Church has mistakenly believed that if satanic assaults on our minds, bodies, and spirits are ignored, these influences will just disappear. Unfortunately, this is not so. Almost every Christian has been repeatedly urged to build his spiritual strength, and most make a few halfhearted attempts and then give up. They haven't sensed the spiritual battle around them.[32] Believers need to be protected. If this threat to us believers is legitimate, and I believe it is, then what the Army calls "force protection" measures must be aggressively undertaken and sustained by the Church. Believers must seek creative ways to strengthen, heal, and if necessary, provide deliverance for Christian soldiers.

As previously mentioned, both my wife and I were ushered into the Charismatic Renewal Movement in 1970. We both received what was then known as "the baptism of the Holy Spirit" with a manifestation of the gift of tongues. I entered Fuller Seminary in the late summer of 1971. At that time, there were many Master of Divinity students who were "neo-Pentecostal." Apart from the existence of charismatic prayer groups, the seminary's course of study was very traditional. It was not until the late '70s or early '80s that Fuller Seminary directly exposed students and faculty to the reality of the charismatic movement.

The popular but controversial seminary course MC510, "Signs, Wonders and Church Growth," offered during the winter quarter of 1982, caused a significant upheaval. My former professors, C. Peter Wagner and Charles Kraft, were profoundly influenced during this period. While not aware of their spiritual pilgrimage prior to and during this period, I later received their testimonies as a Doctor of Ministry student during the late '90s. I was struck by their complete personal and theological transformation. Their holy boldness in pursuing a noticeably "militant" Christianity was astonishing. Both of them during the '90s would develop church renewal and healing/deliverance ministries.

Stemming from reactions to Third World students' enrollment in the seminary's church growth courses, Donald A. McGavran became convinced that something must be done to understand the mounting worldwide evidence concerning "signs and wonders." The seminary course evolved into a popular manual published by *Christian Life Magazine* in October 1982. In the book's introduction, the editors recount the following piece of church history:

> After a long period of decline, a renewal of these signs and wonders is appearing in both Protestant and Catholic Church circles. For the most part, this emergence of spiritual life has stemmed from the grassroots, not from ecclesiastical or theological sources. Groups of believers—sometimes led by a single courageous pastor, sometimes not—have provided the launching pad from which the Holy Spirit has moved. The renaissance first began early in the 20th century. But not until the early 1950's did it surface in the historic Protestant denominations; in the early 1960's in the Roman Catholic Church.[33]

Although this account in 1982 is stirring and instructive, what has transpired during these last twenty-two years? In 2003, we find a dramatic polarization between many historic, mainstream churches and the incredible rise of the nondenominational church. While the so-called Third Wave Movement of the Church continues to develop, many mainstream churches seem hopelessly mired in years of membership decline and what some would call apostasy. The "lightning-rod" issue of homosexuality, indeed aberrant sexuality in general, is draining the life out of many historic Protestant churches. The recent consecration of an openly homosexual Episcopal bishop in the New Hampshire diocese may cause a permanent split in that body. The Roman Catholic controversy over pedophile priests poses a severe threat to their church's vitality. Many had hoped for a national religious revival several years ago, yet, according to a January 1998 George Barna survey, no such revival materialized as the American church moved into the next century.

> God and faith are still hot, but long-term or intense religious commitments are not. Despite their fascination with spirituality, most churched people are only moderately devoted to their current church and they are not deeply invested in spiritual growth. It seems that many adults are awaiting the next big spiritual fad to explore. The breadth of our intrigue with faith remains much more extensive than the depth of our commitment to genuine spiritual development.[34]

A spiritual intelligence assessment shows that Satan threatens the Church with three primary tactics. The Church is having a difficult time quelling the attacks. First, Satan deceives human beings into thinking and eventually believing he is, as Pagels points out, "a reflection of how we perceive ourselves." This reduces Satanic attacks to mere relational aberrations between people. Second, "spiritual powers" that actually can and do attack human bodies, minds, and spirits cannot be effectively resisted or thwarted. Therefore, fear is rampant and paralyzes many believers to inaction or worse, indifference. Thus, true freedom from personal and congregational bondage is not an option. Lastly, Satan lulls the Church into complacency and convinces believers not to be too enthusiastic about spiritual growth, preferring instead as Barna suggests to "wait for the next big spiritual fad to explore." C.S. Lewis' Uncle Screwtape describes to Wormwood this "law of undulation" in the following passage:

Humans are amphibians—half spirit and half animal. (The Enemy's [i.e. God's] determination to produce such a revolting hybrid was one of the things that determined Our Father [i.e. Satan] to withdraw his support from Him.) As spirits they belong to the eternal world, but as animals they inhabit time. This means that while their spirit can be directed to an eternal object, their bodies, passions, and imaginations are in continual change, for to be in time means to change. Their nearest approach to constancy, therefore, is undulation—the repeated return to a level from which they repeatedly fall back, a series of troughs and peaks...The dryness and dullness through which your patient is now going are not, as you fondly suppose, your workmanship; they are merely a natural phenomenon which will do us no good unless you make good use of it.[35]

Taking and holding the enemy's ground means the Church must find ways of reconnecting with its only power source—namely, the Holy Spirit. In 1982, Fuller Seminary discovered that when it balanced the rationalistic approach of education with a more experiential, relational approach, many people were blessed and healed. I remember even in the early '70s that many Master of Divinity students were extremely interested in the gifts of the Spirit and the charismatic movement. The seminary's "Signs and Wonders" course was probably the most popular course offered. In the first chapter of the course manual, *Signs and Wonders for Today*, the editors make this statement: "The Book of Acts is no museum piece. It is a dynamic guidebook as to how the Gospel of Jesus, accompanied by the power of the Holy Spirit, penetrates new territory. When Jesus sent out His disciples for the first time, He told them not only to preach that the kingdom of God is at hand, but also to heal the sick, cleanse the lepers, raise the dead and cast out demons." (Matthew 10: 7-8) [36]How did Jesus expect the disciples to "penetrate new territory?" Satan loves to prevent the Church's expansion by any means. He will aggressively block any moves of God into his area of interest or operation.

The Controversy Surrounding Territorial Spirits and Spiritual Mapping

The last step in the IPB process is the analysis of enemy COAs. What will the enemy do, and when will he do it? Knowing the location of the enemy is important in deciding how one will engage him. The overriding motivation is to remove an enemy from a territory one wishes to occupy and to rescue any friendly forces present. Comparing the Old Testament's Davidic and Danielic, James Kallas believes that Jesus' whole purpose was to bring restoration and wholeness. In effect, Jesus engaged in a cosmic rescue operation. "Whereas the man in the street looked for a Davidic empire in which the Jew would be freed of the Roman, Jesus, on the contrary, was speaking of the Danielic hope, an otherworldly kingdom, a cleansed cosmos."[37] If Kallas is correct, and I believe he is, then Jesus' actions as the paramount spiritual warrior are to be imitated. To put it bluntly, there's a whole lot of cleaning left to do in this world! People need healing of their bodies, minds, and spirits. They need the hope of sins forgiven, and many need deliverance from demons. Kallas continues:

> Salvation, freedom, rescue, being wrenched free from this evil power: this is the view from which the great gospel word *sozo* comes, rescue from Satan, restoration unto wholeness. From this point of view the emphasis upon the nature of God would stress, not his love, but his power. It is the superiority of God that counts. He is stronger than Satan and able to set man free. It is not that God's love is unimportant. If he were not love, he would not attempt our rescue.[38]

The great watchword then is "rescue." Jesus desires more than anything else our wholeness and effective witness. The ultimate goal in the words of John the Baptist is for people to "repent and believe in the gospel" (Mark 1:15, NASV). The question becomes how to mount the rescue operations needed to free billions of people so they can hear and respond to the Gospel message

Several years ago, someone suggested I read Frank Peretti's new book, *This Present Darkness*. I read it with fascination, and I also read his two sequels. These books caught the Christian community's attention because they provided a plausible description and motivation to deliver families, churches, and communities from Satan. Peretti asserted that combative prayer would enable Christians to carry out the Great Commission with unparalleled success and defeat demonic attack. Spurred on by the bestselling novels of Frank Peretti with lurid descriptions of grotesque, sulfur-spewing demons circling small towns, threatening children, and overthrowing elected governments, many Christians have awakened to the reality of spiritual warfare.[39] Many Christians sincerely desire to wage a more aggressive war against what Paul terms "principalities and powers." The so-called spiritual warfare network of churches has developed an ambitious strategy of waging a spiritually relentless war. The network has issued a bold call to arms!

A professor at Singapore Bible College named Chuck Lowe has written a very complete and sometimes scathing critique of C. Peter Wagner's so-called "Strategic Level Spiritual Warfare" (SLSW) movement. Lowe accurately summarizes what SLSW is all about in the following passage:

> Strategic level spiritual warfare seeks to remedy the casual, take-it-for granted approach to spiritual warfare characteristic of traditional evangelicalism. The new warfare engages in detailed analysis of the enemy and his methods of operation, identifies the chinks in his armor, and develops a strategy to defeat him. This new methodology has captured the popular imagination and is making considerable inroads into missionary thinking and strategy...Books are written by the dozen, seminars held around the world, study groups formed, marches scheduled, all with one purpose: to disarm the spiritual powers of wickedness that impede the spread of the Gospel.[40]

Lowe concedes that as a result of the SLSW proponents' efforts, tremendous enthusiasm for prayer has swept many churches. Lowe views the results as "extraordinary," and they are indeed. While participating in another Doctor of Ministry course entitled "Churches in the New Apostolic Paradigm" in July 1998, I learned firsthand about the amazing plans to construct a World Prayer Center on the grounds of the New Life Church in Colorado Springs, Colorado. Here was the heart of the new SLSW movement. I saw and heard C. Peter Wagner, the professor of the course and Ted Haggard, Pastor of New Life Church, describe their vision. Taking a tour of the Center in the summer of 1998, I was awed. I believe that all in the class could not help but be impressed with the faith, vision, and missionary zeal of Wagner, Haggard, and their colleagues. With all this new energy for missions, Lowe is not at all convinced that SLSW advocates are correct in their theological foundation and operational techniques. He says: "But having awakened to the reality of the spiritual battle, many are apprehensive. How can so few win against so many? How shall mere mortals defeat demons?"[41]

In effect, the World Prayer Center in Colorado has become a spiritual battle command center. In all armies, soldiers in the field must have confidence in their commanders if they are to carry out their operational orders. Chuck Lowe seriously questions whether Wagner is actually teaching sound Bible doctrine or harming the whole Church. Lowe and others believe that Wagner's group needs a serious investigation. Here is the crux of the problem: "SLSW consumes enormous resources in money, time and personnel, sending people on expensive short-term prayer journeys around the world, and teaching residential personnel to engage in extraordinary detailed mapping of entire neighborhoods, down to the type and colour of housing on each street."[42] The clear implication is that SLSW may represent an easier, more efficient way to conduct traditional cross-cultural evangelism. What I hear these critics saying is essentially this: Why should the Church risk diverting its limited resources on a scheme that is not solidly biblical? I also sense that there may be a bit of theological jealousy.

In a CNN newscast on 6 November 2003, General Richard Myers, Chairman of the Joint Chiefs of Staff, said that one of the primary benefits in training and deploying larger numbers of Iraqi policemen was that the police would possess more "situational awareness."

Situational awareness is a concept that, in this case, asserts that a spiritual intelligence assessment is required to research, catalog, and plan future biblical combat operations. It is exactly this concept that motivates SLSW adherents to attempt to engage in "spiritual mapping" of demon-infested geographical regions of the world. The idea to "map" certain regions resistant to the Gospel creates spiritual pressure so that what Paul calls "spiritual forces of wickedness in heavenly places" (Ephesians 6: 12, NASV) are disarmed.

Part of the argument with the SLSW is that it over states the organizational makeup of the demonic hierarchy. The Pauline term "heavenly places" in SLSW theology denotes a tight labyrinth of a demonic chain of command that must and presumably can be disrupted. There is no question that demonic forces are well placed. The sphere of the activity of evil spirits extends over the whole universe, including "the heavenlies." (*ta epourania*) This is made quite explicit in Ephesians 6: 12, which speaks about "superhuman forces of evil in the heavens" (*epourania*).[43] William Barclay's commentary on this verse is very instructive in that it opposes the literal demonic hierarchy and is content to leave the specifics ambiguous.

> Undoubtedly life was much more terrifying for the ancient people than it is for us today. They believed implicitly in evil spirits, who filled the air and were determined to work men harm. The words which Paul uses, powers, authorities, world-rulers, are all names for different classes of these evil spirits. To him the whole universe was a battleground...We may not take Paul's actual language literally; but our experience will tell us that there is an active power of evil in the world.[44]

I believe Barclay's comment begs the question. It appears he wants it both ways! He tells us not to take Paul literally and then reminds the reader that we should listen and learn from our own experience. Walter Wink, on the other hand, is enamored of elaborate discussions of "worldviews." He states, "When people tell of their experiences of evil in the world, they often lapse into the language of the ancient worldview. Demons and angels are depicted as separate beings soaring about in the sky rather than as the spirituality of institutions and systems." [45]We are left with the question: are there actual demonic forces at work in a concerted way or not? The Bible's evidence is overwhelmingly affirmative. Advocates of SLSW take the discussion further by asserting a well-organized demonic hierarchy that, if understood and "mapped," can be thwarted.

Charles Kraft outlines six principles that, in his words, offer "a very preliminary attempt to figure out some of the principles of spirit-world, human-world interaction. I will attempt here to list some of the things we think we have learned." [46]Having taken this class, I appreciated how Kraft was careful to couch his conclusions with terms like "think" and "seem." Kraft's sixth principle is the most relevant to our discussion. It reads:

Principle 6: Territories and Organizations Can Be Subject to Spirit Power

> 1.1 Cosmic level spirits seem to exert what might be referred to as a "force field" influence over territories, buildings and organizations, including nations
> 1.2 In order for spirit beings to have authority over territories and organizations, they must have legal rights
> 1.3 The rules for breaking the power of dedication over territories are parallel to those for breaking such power over individuals
> 1.4 Cosmic level spirits seem to wield their authority over territories as defined by humans
> 1.5 There seem to be cosmic level spirits that are in charge of organizations, institutions and activities
> 1.6 There are rules that can be followed to launch attacks upon evil spirits assigned to territories and organizations[47]

The hermeneutical problems are significant with these points, according to Chuck Lowe. Specifically, Lowe contends that the advocates of SLSW misuse and misinterpret Scripture and make sweeping inferences that are harmful to the peace and purity of the Church. The main verse dealing with so-called "ruling spirits" is in Daniel 10:13. It deals with the archangel Michael's recounting of the "Prince of Persia," who thwarted Daniel's prayers and the archangel himself for twenty-one days. Michael tells Daniel that, "the prince of the kingdom of Persia was withstanding me twenty-one days." (NASV) Kraft does indeed make this verse central to his demonic hierarchy argument.[48] Lowe responds:

> From this text proponents of SLSW infer the existence of an entire hierarchy of demons ruling over territories of various sizes...This argument infers a lot out of a little. From demonic rulers over two nations, to demonic rulers over all nations, to demonic rulers over smaller units within each nation. Timothy Warner is right to call this hypothesis an assumption; actually it is an assumption built on an analogy and leading to an inference. Where evidence exists, assumption and inference are unnecessary.[49]

These issues are academic but relevant to any credible spiritual intelligence gathering effort. Certainly, demonic forces are intelligent. They speak, reason, and are clear in their mission to hinder the Gospel and harass believers. To go into more detail concerning Wagner and Kraft's critics would exceed the scope of this book. I believe that Scripture, while shedding some light on these issues, does not provide all the information we may want. As a new Christian, I learned one cardinal principal: Scripture interprets experience, not the reverse! If we go beyond what the Bible says, we do so at our own peril. At a minimum, we can learn to be more intentional about our work and witness. This effort requires leadership that knows the objective.

PART III: LEADING THE FORCE

CHAPTER FOUR

What Leadership Means in the U.S. Army

The United States Army values leaders and spends enormous amounts of time and resources studying leadership and cultivating it at all levels. When considering what leadership means, I remember the leaders I have served with for more than twenty years. Most of my senior commanders and non-commissioned officers have been highly skilled in their particular military occupational specialty. These commanders have been somewhat successful at instilling confidence and maintaining unit morale. According to the Army Field Manual 22-100, "Leadership is the process of influencing others to accomplish the mission by providing purpose, direction, and motivation."[1] In a companion document for senior leaders, Army Field Manual 22-103 says, "Leadership and command at senior levels is the art of direct and indirect influence and the skill of creating the conditions for sustained organizational success to achieve the desired results."[2] At the lower levels of command, one can see that the emphasis is on directly influencing individuals, whereas at higher levels of command, there is an expected shift at a more indirect and overall organizational responsibility.

When I first entered active duty, I was assigned to the newly reactivated Tenth Mountain Division (Light Infantry) at Fort Drum, New York. The commanding general at that time was Peter J. Boylan. I have kept through the years his "ten commandments" of leadership. General Boylan stated:

(1) You are not here for the money; (2) Integrity is nonnegotiable; (3) If it does not improve combat readiness, why do it? (4) If you do not take care of your soldiers, nobody else will; (5) The chain of command works...if you use it; (6) Do not do your subordinates' work; (7) Never mind whose fault it is; get it fixed; (8) Surprises are for birthdays; (9) Keep things in perspective and (10) If you rarely laugh, you are in the wrong line of work.[3]

All of these "commandments" and quotations from field manuals are good in theory. The real value of a leader of course is seen and known during war. In a war, situations are far from concrete or by the book. Leaders during combat must be able to "assess the situation and form their battlefield vision. Second, those at senior levels have a high tolerance for ambiguity and uncertainty."[4] While Army doctrine—i.e. regulations, field manuals, Department of the Army pamphlets, etc.—are commendable and usually well written, it is the actual personal life examples of commanders that soldiers will remember and follow. I must, in all candor, say that in my experience of twenty years, most commanders (officers) and command sergeant majors (senior enlisted persons) have not shown they can handle what FM 22-103 calls "a high tolerance for ambiguity and uncertainty." If anything, my senior leaders demanded absolute clarity and would not abide by any confusion! Command climate surveys or "sensing sessions" periodically directed by higher headquarters usually reveal some common problems. The realities of "careerism" and the brutal competitiveness for promotion have sustained, in my opinion, a "zero defect" Army. Reluctant to take career-risks, many Army leaders have succumbed to more managerial roles rather than mentor roles. "Management activities often seem to dominate."[5] The Army, in my experience, does not like to hear this, but it is true—

even in the Chaplain Corps. I want to concentrate on the Army's theory of leadership and raise some challenges for the Church.

Leadership is really the key to everything the Army does. When commanders take the guidon of the unit, they assume the first-line responsibility for all soldiers and their families. The guidon symbolizes all that the unit has been and done during peace and war since its activation. The company level is where soldiers develop their unit identity. They adopt a slogan, a mascot, and a fighting spirit. An example of an initial company commander "pep talk memorandum" follows:

> Soldiers want to be on a winning team. After all, losing in combat leads to death. Our mission as the leaders of this company is to build a winning team. Leadership is the force behind all the things that make winning possible. If you imagine a winning team as a wheel, leadership based on values and principles is the hub that powers the wheel, while the spokes are discipline, fitness, and motivation.[6]

Company commanders and first sergeants model the behavior that is expected of every soldier and enable the troops to "train as they will fight." Training that is not realistic and related to the unit's wartime mission is peripheral. Soldiers want to do what they volunteered to do—that is, learn their MOS and where they will fit into the war-fighting scheme of the army. The leadership must never forget that they and their soldiers are one order away from war. Commanders who get caught up in what are called "training distracters" (i.e. training interruptions) fail their soldiers because their soldiers will not be able to perform and survive in combat. "Commanding one hundred and twenty soldiers, potentially in combat, is a responsibility that is quite humbling if you stop to think about it. It is an extremely challenging, sometimes lonely experience that will test your mettle, give you incredible satisfaction, and push you beyond your abilities."[7]

My present unit had a subordinate company whose commander had done poorly in command. He was blamed for the unit's very low morale and stepped down after only one year instead of having a normal eighteen-month tour of duty. He failed in communicating a vision to his soldiers and Department of the Army civilians (DACs). Morale and esprit are very low. People don't believe his message because they don't believe him! I have seen many tyrannical officers and senior enlisted persons advance in rank while many caring and soldier-oriented leaders are bypassed. Many are promoted because of their operational skills but are not in tune with their subordinates' concerns or feelings. The important balance between war-fighting competency and people-oriented behavior is often out of synch within the Army's leadership.

To define leadership as the art of inspiring the spirit and act of following may be simple enough in theory, but what enables a leader to accomplish this? How does a person develop the ability to become a leader? Are leaders born or made? Ultimately a theory of leadership begins with an assumption about human nature. While it is commonplace to discuss human nature in terms of fundamentally good, bad, or a "blank slate," a number of ancient philosophers had a slightly different perspective. They saw people in terms of what they can be and should be...The study of leadership necessarily begins with a concept of humanity.[8]

Seven Core Values

The Army appeals to aspects of "humanness" in its training of enlisted soldiers and newly commissioned officers. A big part of the so-called "soldierization" process is the inculcation of seven core values into the lives of America's soldiers. By design, the Army five or six years ago developed an easily memorized leadership tool to link these core values with what it hopes to instill into the force. The acrostic "LDRSHIP" delineates the values of loyalty, duty, respect, selfless service, honor, integrity, and personal courage. These core values are routinely written on many official communications and painted on walls, steps, and other common areas at basic training installations and every Army post in the world. Soldiers are required to know and recite them when asked by their drill sergeants. In fact, there is a plastic "credit card" and a smaller metal "dog tag" that soldiers are directed to always have on their person. The Army NCO Guide in 1986 specified why values are important: "Values are ideas about worth and importance of things, concepts and people. They come from beliefs. They influence priorities...The more you build these traits in yourself and others, the more successful you will be." An army must establish and maintain discipline. This inner resolve creates a warrior ethos.

Former Sergeant Major of the Army, William G. Bainbridge, expresses the sentiment thus: "The core of a soldier is moral discipline. It is intertwined with the discipline of physical and mental achievement. It motivates doing on your own what is right without prodding...It is an inner critic that refuses to tolerate less than your best."[9] The bedrock of the United States Army is its emphasis on developing a warrior ethos that emanates from these seven core values.

The Warrior Ethos and the Leadership Art

Doing one's best for a soldier means being a warrior. The warrior mentality for the United States Army is its soul. Although all soldiers are trained in basic soldier skills, not all soldiers are considered members of the "combat arms." Traditionally, combat arms MOS's are infantry, armor, and artillery. However, most of the Army's soldiers are members of two other branch groupings—combat support or combat service support. Soldiers with occupational specialties in the signal corps, combat engineers, ordnance, military intelligence, quartermaster, finance, adjutant general, and others support the so-called "trigger-pullers" in the combat arms. Obviously, there are far more support functions in the army than there are direct combat branches. The current issue is that in the Army, these "support" soldiers need to be more motivated and ready for direct combat.

This important issue came into the public awareness when Private First Class (PFC) Jessica Lynch's maintenance unit came under attack in Iraq in March 2003. PFC Lynch's unit was physically separated from the main body. They were brutally attacked by Iraqis. PFC Lynch and her fellow soldiers were apparently not completely prepared for the attack. In the aftermath of this event, the new Army Chief of Staff, General Schoomaker, directed that in the future all soldiers, regardless of their branch, receive more frequent and intensive weapons training and more rigorous hand-to-hand combat training. The stated rationale is to elevate the warrior ethos in the United States Army. As General Schoomaker was sworn in as Chief of Staff, he stated, "War is both a physical reality and a state of mind. War is ambiguous, uncertain, and unfair. When we are at war, we must think and act differently. We become more flexible and more adaptable. We must anticipate the ultimate reality check: combat."[10]

More soldiers need to be, in effect, re-stimulated as warriors. The Marines, by comparison, have always maintained the philosophy that every marine, regardless of what their MOS is, is considered a rifleman first of all. While stationed at APG (an Army post), as a brigade chaplain, I became acquainted with the Marine mentality. Marines are, historically, the first armed force that closes with the enemy. General Schoomaker seeks to instill in the Army this same ethos. I remember seeing a beautiful color circular at APG entitled "The Warrior Ethos." The document was required reading for all members of the Training and Doctrine Command (TRADOC). The circular stated that, "The Warrior Ethos is the sum of the distinguishing characteristics that describe what it means to be a soldier, a soldier committed to, and prepared to close with and kill or capture the enemy." The "Warrior Ethos" is:

> The self-discipline to harden one's body and soul through demanding physical training and exertion; The belief that one's word is one's bond and that trust binds soldiers together to risk life and limb; The mental toughness to endure, without compliant, the extremes of weather and lack of sleep and food; The embodiment "to guard my post until properly relieved"; The iron-will, determination, and confidence to overcome all odds, even in seemingly hopeless situations; The relentless desire to be the best, to be a winner, but never at the expense of one's comrades or unit; The uncompro-

mising commitment to be technically and tactically competent, to achieve and exceed demanding standards; to be combat ready; The inherent selflessness to give your last ounce of water to your men and your buddy; to replace "me" with "we"; The unqualified willingness to sacrifice oneself for the mission, the unit or a comrade; The ability to overcome the horrors of battle-death, wounds, fear—to cross "the killing ground" under fire, even as the lone survivor; To always put the mission, the unit and the country first and oneself second; To never give up, to never give in, to never be satisfied with anything short of victory.[11]

It might seem strange to suggest that the United States Army needs a revision of its "warrior ethos," but it does. Any armed force periodically must refocus its personnel so that they are kept honed and ready for any mission. Not only are weapons systems, and force structure being included in the Army Transformation program, but also the concepts and practice of leadership itself. Effective leaders are ready students of history.

Leadership Lessons from the Army's History

One creative army unit recently implemented a leadership initiative concentrating on some remarkable lessons from the historic expedition of Lewis and Clarke. This innovative course of study not only focused on the journey's logistics but, more importantly, on how decisions were conceived and executed. In short, this leadership-training program seeks to elicit the leadership art. A leadership team must be agile and adaptive. In December 2003, the Army's new "Stryker" brigade joined Operation Iraqi Freedom. It is this unit that attempted to internalize the leadership lessons of this famous westward expedition of 1803-1806.

One of the Army's newest units, the second Stryker Brigade Combat Team, has reached 200 years into the past for lessons in agile and adaptive leadership...Col. Bob Brown, commander of the 1st Brigade, 25th Infantry Division at Fort

Lewis, Washington said the Lewis and Clark Expedition of 1803-06 was so replete with examples of good leadership that he and his staff fashioned a training event around it... Each of the officers and NCO's was assigned to one of 22 squads...The soldiers recreated many of the activities noted by the explorers in their journals 200 years ago—desalinization, portage, etc.—and discussed how the teamwork and other qualities of the exercise still fits in today's Army.[12]

A leader's ability to foster teamwork is the critical component needed in order to wage war or build peace. The United States Army prior to World War II was an Army that lacked equipment, ammunition, aircraft, and most importantly, personnel. The monumental task facing the Nation's leadership eventually fell on General Dwight D. Eisenhower ("Ike"), who quickly became the Supreme Allied Commander. Ike valued and inspired teamwork. The force of his personality demonstrated various traits essential to victory. He retained the winning traits of authenticity, vigor, and integrity. One British general marveled, "One of the fascinations of the war was to see how Americans developed their great men so quickly. None more than Eisenhower."[13]

His talent for creating and projecting visionary "command truths" was also eventually displayed to Allied leaders. Without question, the decision to lead, plan, and conduct the invasion of the European continent was one of the greatest keys to ending the war. In considering who would lead the invasion and become operation overlord, a laborious decision-making process debated "Ike's" personal and command qualities. While he did not have a "well-developed strategic grasp required for global war planning," there were other considerations.[14] Ike had demonstrated an extraordinary diplomatic talent for getting allied generals and admirals to work in harness. In this chairman of the board capacity, by and large, he earned the respect of the British. Diplomacy was the overriding talent required of the overlord commander, and no American general had it in greater abundance than Ike.[15]

Another great commander, General George S. Patton, did not possess diplomacy but, on the other hand, was one of America's greatest battlefield generals. Although almost fired several times by Ike, Patton exhibited combat leadership that was arguably unequaled and indispensable. Despite numerous serious personal flaws, "Ike insisted on Patton for his undeniable drive" on the battlefield.[16]

Patton's war-fighting leadership exhibited an aggressive, no-nonsense style that many soldiers both admired and disdained. Major General William A. Cohen commented, "He was tough. War is tough. Leaders have to be tough. He drove his army hard, yes, and he made many enemies among colleagues and subordinates, but he also produced results. He was indeed arrogant, but sometimes a good leader has to be larger than life."[17] In the preface to a Patton biography, New York Yankee owner George Steinbrenner III comments about the general: "I consider General George S. Patton, with all his controversy, idiosyncrasies, and unpredictability, to be perhaps the greatest of them all, 'the ultimate warrior.'"[18] How did this "ultimate warrior" approach leadership?

> Patton's leadership lessons ring true today as they did when he was leading the Third Army across France and into Germany itself. His enduring message is one of preparation, teamwork, pride, motivation, and discipline—never asking his men to do anything that he himself would not do...

> Patton could reduce complex tasks to their essence, then, focus all of his resources on that essence. He believed in attention to every detail. Put all the pieces in place, give your people every opportunity to succeed, and they will do so. Give people goals they can understand, they will meet them. Set the bar high and your people will raise themselves to meet it.[19]

By putting "all the pieces in place," Patton exemplified the qualities of a master strategist. Warrior-leaders like Eisenhower and Patton understood that combat theories are useless unless they translate into ground maneuver.

Although some of Patton's detractors called him "reckless," he actually was a very careful and studious planner. He was a student of his opposition and their leadership. Before making a decision, he would gather all the facts he could and seek input from trusted advisors. He would study the appointed task from many angles, trying to spot the pitfalls as well as the advantages of various strategies.[20]

Strategic and Tactical Insights

Carl Von Clausewitz book, *On War*, was the most significant attempt in Western history to understand war, both in its internal dynamics and as an instrument of policy. It has been read throughout the world and has stimulated generations of soldiers, statesman, and intellectuals such as Marx, Bismarck, Churchill, and Hitler.[21] In this book, Clausewitz focuses on the strategy of war fighting to the exclusion of a discussion on tactics. What exactly is strategy? Clausewitz says, "Strategy is the use of the engagement for the purpose of the war. The strategist must therefore define an aim for the entire war... In other words, he will draft the plan of the war, and the aim will determine the series of actions intended to achieve it. Clausewitz stresses that the most important objective in a campaign is the destruction of the opposing army..."[22] The great end or "aim" is the strategy.

Strategy depends for success, first and most, on a sound *calculation and co-ordination of the end and the means*. The end must be proportioned to the total means...[23]

Most military historians would agree that Napoleon was a master strategist. The "end" was always on his mind. He was calculating, yet bold on the battlefield. Napoleon was not afraid to try new approaches. He developed something called a "distributed strategic advance." Until the eighteenth century, a physically concentrated advance (to the battlefield) and a tactical advance (*on* the battlefield) was the rule. Then Napoleon, exploiting Bourcet's ideas and the new divisional system, introduced a *distributed strategic advance*—the army moving in independent fractions.[24] This great military conqueror believed a new method of conducting war was necessary. Because new industrial conditions existed, Napoleon devised what was called the *dispersed strategic advance*. Several variations of dispersal could be chosen.

(i) Dispersed advance with concentrated single aim, i.e. against one objective;

(ii) Dispersed advance with concentrated serial aim, i.e. against successive objectives;

(iii) Dispersed advance with distributed aim, i.e. against a number of objectives simultaneously.[25]

This development of strategy during the French Revolution allowed armies to "aim at permeating and dominating areas rather than capturing lines; at the practicable object of paralyzing the enemy's action rather than the theoretical object of crushing his forces."[26]

It is important to also differentiate between strategy and tactics. While strategy concerns itself with the effect on the big picture, tactics focuses on the actual fighting, i.e. "the dispositions for and control of such direct action... Tactics is an application of strategy on a lower plane."[27]

Military leaders at all levels have a solemn responsibility to remain technically and tactically proficient. How an enemy or even a *potential* enemy fights is knowledge that is acquired through leveraging the actual combat experience of soldiers and constantly refining battlefield simulations. The Army FM 22-103 states, "For leaders and commanders, this entails firm knowledge of an understanding how the tactical, operational and strategic levels of warfare apply to organizations and units, regardless of their current assignment."[28] The extensive use of battle simulators provides a renewable laboratory that refines lessons in command and control for the Army.

The Dynamics of Command and Control

While it is true that the United States Army has its flaws, the theoretical and operational concepts of Command and Control (C2) it exercises are, in my experience, quite efficient. In essence, the basic concept may be defined as "...The exercise of authority and direction by a properly designated commander over assigned and attached forces in the accomplishment of the mission. Command and control functions are performed through an arrangement of personnel, equipment, communications, facilities, and procedures employed by a commander in planning, directing, coordinating, and controlling forces and operations in the accomplishment of the mission."[29] As a war-fighting entity, the Army has critical information requirements. The army institution differentiates between command and control, thereby achieving complete situational awareness.

Command is the authoritative act of making decisions and ordering action; *control* is the act of monitoring and influencing this action. The commander cannot command effectively without control, and he, with or without the staff, cannot exercise control without command.

The commander uses command and control, which includes the staff, to make effective decisions, to manage the uncertainty of combat, to employ military forces effi-ciently... In short, the goal of command and control is mission accomplishment, while the object of command and control is forces. The staff is the most important resource that the commander uses to exercise missions.[30]

In the Army, a commander's staff can make or break them. It is the staff that plans, coordinates, and executes all missions. Staff officers at the battalion, which is the basic operational level, include the executive Officer (XO), the Personnel Officer (S-1), the Security Officer (S-2), the Operations Officer (S-3), and the Logistics Officer (S-4). In the last dozen years, another basic staff member, the S-6, has been added to supervise and direct all automated systems—

namely computer systems. The unit chaplain is also assigned to the commander's special staff. Depending on the kind of unit at levels above battalion, more special staff is authorized. There may be a doctor, lawyer, psychiatrist, or social worker. These various staff members provide crucial planning capabilities for the commander as the unit conducts peacetime or wartime missions. However, all army units and their staffs must always focus on being prepared for war.

Although ultimate authority, responsibility, and accountability rest wholly with the commander, he can delegate specific authority to staff officers to decide and to act within their own areas of responsibility. Each subordinate staff officer must understand authority, responsibility, and accountability as they relate to his relationship with the commander, other staff officers, and subordinate commanders. Most important, the staff member must always remember that he is there to support and assist his commander.[31]

I have been privileged to serve with commanders who exercised both exceptionally fine and exceptionally poor leadership. No one would question these commanders' authority to command. However, there are two kinds of authority. There is statutory authority, and there is moral authority. For soldiers, there is a world of difference between the two! Soldiers quickly make value judgments in two areas about their commanders. First, is the commander competent in his or her military occupational specialty? That is, is he or she skilled in the special "science" of their branch? Second, does the commander possess troop-leading and communication skills? Is he or she able to relate and inspire people? Here is the "art" of command:

Command is the art of decision making and of leading and motivating soldiers and their organizations into action to impose the Nation's will over the enemy and accomplish missions at the least expense in manpower and material. Command is vested in an individual who has total responsibility. The essence of command is defined by the commander's competence, intuition, judgment, initiative, and character, *and* (italics mine) his ability to inspire and gain the trust of his unit.[32]

The goal of "control" for an army unit is to make decisions faster than the enemy. In the heat of the battlefield, a commander and the staff desire to achieve complete situational awareness (SA). Control is based on situational information, such as mission, enemy, terrain, troops, and time available (METT-T) from all sources. The commander uses this information to adjust the resources, concept, or objective of the plan, or to exploit success in operations.[33] The staff assists in exercising control by:

(1) Acquiring and supplying means to accomplish the commander's intent
(2) Defining limits
(3) Determining requirements
(4) Allocating means
(5) Monitoring status and performance and reporting significant changes to the commander
(6) Developing specific guidance from general guidance
(7) Forecasting change.[34]

In the final analysis, leadership is about relating to and influencing people. In my experience, Army commanders are proficient at the science but not the art of war. Many of my commanders have projected an image of careerism. Speaking about his experience at West Point, retired General Norman Schwarzkopf summarizes the essence of leadership: "Some officers spend all their time currying favor and worrying about the next promotion, a miserable way to live. But West Point saved me from that by instilling the ideal of service above self. It gave me far more than a military career, it gave me a calling."[35]

CHAPTER FIVE

THE BIBLICAL PICTURES
OF LEADERSHIP

There is a vast difference between command and effective leadership. The Army endeavors to teach and, more importantly, model effective leadership, but often fails because of rampant careerism. The "rank" of an officer or senior enlisted person can often corrupt leaders into thinking more of themselves than they should. Reminiscing about recent Army generals, former Army Chief of Staff Eric Shinseki provides a wonderful insight that is, in itself, Biblical:

> These leaders (former generals) rose to their enormous task because they understood the important distinction between command and effective leadership. They taught us that command is about authority, about an appointment to a position, a set of orders granting title. Effective leadership is different. It must be learned and practiced in order for it to rise to the level of art. It has to do with values internalized and the willingness to sacrifice or subordinate all other concerns-advancement, personal wellbeing, safety-for others... You must love those you lead before you can be an effective leader. You can certainly command without that sense of commitment, but you cannot lead without it;

and without leadership, command is a hollow experience—a vacuum often filled with mistrust and arrogance.[1]

In light of the Army's leadership model outlined in chapter four, what kind of leadership template is revealed in Scripture? Can the Church benefit from military concepts and practice? Are there points of army doctrine that are relevant to the personal faith practices of believers today and instructive in the advancement of the Gospel in the twenty-first century? How does the ultimate spiritual warrior, Jesus, understand "command" and "authority?"

The Leadership Example of Jesus

The time-honored Army tradition of leadership transition is called "The Change of Command" ceremony. Soldiers know that when the unit colors are passed to the new commander, there will be change. Even before Jesus fully enters the scene and "takes command," John the Baptist, His predecessor and advance man, paints an impressive word-picture that influences the crowds so that they would transfer loyalty to Jesus. John says, "…but He who is coming after me is mightier than I, and I am not fit to remove His sandals; He will baptize you with the Holy Spirit and fire." (Matthew 3:11, NIV) For soldiers in the United States Army, "leadership" according to FM 22-100, is "influencing others to accomplish the mission." John takes the opportunity in the closing remarks of his tenure to influence and elicit new loyalties from the people. He hopes that the masses will, in fact, receive and adopt the new mission and their new "commander."

The first prerequisite for a leader, especially a spiritual one, is the issue of truth. In the small but powerful book, *The Leadership Lessons of Jesus,* the authors highlight the importance of truth. Before people can be persuaded to follow a potential leader, they need to know that this leader knows and speaks the truth! The co-authors state, "The relationship between Jesus and John the Baptist demonstrates that truth is always the first and most important element of the spokesperson's message and that a quality spokesperson continues to speak the truth even in tough times when truth may be unpopular."[2]

In this case, the truth John articulates involves a battlefield vision, "a baptism with the Holy Spirit and fire." There can be no misunderstanding at this early juncture that the new commander will lead the people to war! Jesus wastes no time in promoting a new strategic aim. Jesus declares after John had been arrested that, "...the time is fulfilled, and the kingdom of God is at hand; repent and believe the gospel" (Mark 1: 15, NIV). The first lesson Jesus teaches is that He is a general who has been issued orders by the Father to engage in earthly and celestial combat. Jesus wastes no time in recruiting fellow soldiers in this eschatological fight.

With authenticity, vigor, and integrity, Jesus began to expand His leadership influence along the Galilean shore. Additionally, He began cultivating a new "warrior ethos" among the simplest and most unlikely potential recruits. Jesus quickly got the attention of twelve ordinary yet very special men. He called the disciples to be with Him and initiated them into a holy vision. He told them and then showed them about being fishers of men. Providing purpose, direction, and motivation, Jesus provides a paradigm of what discipleship should be like. Obeying orders that didn't make sense, Simon the fisherman was persuaded to cast his net in waters he had fished all night without success. "And when they had done this, they enclosed a great quantity of fish; and their nets began to break...But when Simon saw that, he fell down at Jesus' feet..." (Luke 5: 6; 8, NIV). In effect, Jesus was inviting Simon and the other would-be disciples to climb a ladder leading to a discovery unimagined. In the book *The Ascent of a Leader,* the destiny of the disciple is described. "...Each human being bears the imago *Dei*, the image of God...You have a unique destiny, rooted in who you are, which overflows into all you do and accomplish... A climb of the best kind, this different ladder may scare you at times and cause you to long for safer places while at the same time infusing you with newfound vigor and a pioneering spirit long forgotten."[3] The disciples would come to really need a "pioneering spirit" because Jesus gave them a challenge unlike any other. He said, "Follow me, and I will make you fishers of men." (Matthew 4:19, NIV)

What the Disciples Learned

For more than three years, the disciples followed Jesus. Many of the lessons He taught would not be comprehended for many years to come. Jesus, the ultimate warrior, was also the ultimate commander. He patiently taught His "soldiers" many mysteries and tactical methods. Dietrich Bonhoeffer wrote a letter to former students who were called up for German military service in 1939. He writes that the most important theological lesson focuses on "wonder." The awesome miracle of God made flesh is surely the most significant. The disciples were regularly filled with awe. "Without the holy night there is no theology. 'God revealed in flesh,' the God-man Jesus Christ, is the holy mystery which theology is appointed to guard…It is the task of theology solely to preserve God's wonder as wonder, to understand, to defend, to glorify God's mystery as mystery."[4] To see, understand, and respond to this God made flesh, the disciples shared Simon's plaintive plea, "Depart from me for I am a sinful man, O Lord!" (Luke 5: 8, NIV) The disciples' shock and fear also was a part of their psychological reaction to Jesus. Overwhelmed by his power over the sea they said, "Who is this, that even the wind and sea obey Him?" (Mark 4: 41, NIV) As they saw repeated supernatural demonstrations, the disciples learned the Lord's strategies and tactics.

The issue of authority logically flows out of Jesus' miracles. Without question, true soldiers respond to the great question of "who's in charge?" The only time Scripture records that Jesus was amazed (Matthew 8:10) focuses around the words and heart of the Roman centurion. In Matthew chapter eight, a pagan Roman approached Jesus, begging Him to heal his beloved servant. Extremely self-conscious of his spiritual condition, the centurion tries to discourage Jesus from entering his home. Reminding Jesus of a soldier's understanding of authority, he says, "Lord, I am not worthy for You to come under my roof, but just say the word, and my servant will be healed." (Matthew 8: 8, NIV)

Armies of all nations call their soldiers to recognize and respond to authority. Jesus teaches His charges to do the same, but with a critical difference. He tells them that the rank and position the

world covets is not to be what characterizes them. In their ministries, they are to be men exuding authority without exercising "lordship." (Luke 22: 25, NIV) Comparing Hellenistic monarchs with
the disciples' recurring behavior, Jesus further scolds them about
their frequent ambitions. The word comes from the Latin that means
"canvassing for promotion." Ted Engstrom, in his book *The Making
of a Christian Leader,* comments, "It is true that men can have much
selfish ambition to control others, enjoy power for power's sake, and
be unscrupulous in money-making and the control of other people.
But Jesus gave to the disciples a different standard of ambition and
greatness."[5]

Additionally, the disciples learned what the Army calls "situational awareness" and the importance of METT-T. In Luke 10:1-20,
Jesus "commissions" the seventy to execute a trial mission. In effect,
He tells them to prepare for direct combat with Satan. Like all good
commanders, Jesus reminds His disciples to be aware of everything
around them. They are to proceed in pairs and are ordered to keep
their mission paramount. Jesus says, "Heal those (in whatever city
you enter) who are sick, and say to them, 'The kingdom of God has
come near to you.'" (Luke 10: 9, NIV) In so doing, they are to travel
light (no purse, no bag, and no shoes) and they are to look for opportunities to engage the population in conversation with encouragement. Contrary to an army moving in independent factions, they are
to pursue a "dispersed strategic advance." This strategy will mean
moving against simultaneous objectives.

Scripture does not give us details as to where the disciples went,
but we do know that when they returned with joy after attacking
demonic strongholds, Jesus validated their success by saying, "I was
watching Satan fall from heaven like lightning. Behold, I have given
you authority to tread upon serpents and scorpions, and over all the
power of the enemy..." (Luke 10: 17-19, NIV). Army Field Manual
100-61 entitled, *Armor-and Mechanized-Based Opposing Force
Operational Art* confirms the soundness of Jesus' plan. "Military
planners often divide strategic axes into operational axes. These
are areas that lead to objectives of operational significance, such
as major enemy groupings and/or political and economic centers
that underpin the combat actions of operational forces."[6] Everett

Harrison points out that, "The disciples were able successfully to invade the kingdom of darkness and bring deliverance to many through the power of God shared with them by the Master."[7] By dispersing, the disciples undermined Satan's center of gravity. The Twelve were taught early in Jesus' ministry to strategically advance the kingdom.

How Jesus must have complemented His team! Here was a trial run of what He ordered much later with His Great Commission in Matthew 28. He wanted to instill the notion that the disciples were more effective as a team than as individuals. His little seminary aimed to grow spiritual leaders. Fuller Seminary's former president, David Hubbard, imitated Jesus' example. Hubbard's long-time secretary recalled, "He encouraged people to make decisions. He said it was better to make a wrong decision than to make no decision at all. After a decision was made, he did not criticize. He took the responsibility for his staff's decisions and did not blame them when a decision was wrong. He would review it with them, however, to see what they thought they should do the next time."[8]

The New Apostolic Paradigm

Through its history, the Army is replete with leaders that carried it through war and peace. Great military leaders like Eisenhower and Patton are readily studied and remembered. The Church also remembers its past but must be always ready to share its Master's business. Agile and adaptive church leadership led God's people through persecution and worldwide evangelization efforts. Church leadership, like Army leadership, values commitment and mission accomplishment. Our great Captain, Jesus, provides believers of all ages with the same promise: "And surely I am with you always, to the very end of the age" (Matthew 28: 20b, NIV).

Just as the United States Army is now engaged in its all-encompassing transformation and its goal of attaining the Objective Force, so too must the Church at every level be regularly transforming. The Church's leadership, like the Army's, needs to constantly reassess its effectiveness in accomplishing the mission. Leaders at every level must continually challenge parishioners to cultivate spiritual warrior mentalities.

At its inception, the historic Church moved over the known world with the Gospel and apostolic leadership. C. Peter Wagner states, "The government of the church is based on apostles, prophets, evangelists, pastors and teachers according to Ephesians 4:11. The Bible says, 'And God has appointed these in the church: first apostles, second prophets, third, teachers' (1 Corinthians 12:28, NIV). Apostles are first in order of those with governmental authority."[9] It is believed by some that a new apostolic paradigm is needed in the Church. Wagner's thirteen-year-old ministry, "Global Harvest Ministries," states on its website the following description about the so-called "New Apostolic Reformation:"

> The New Apostolic Reformation is an extraordinary work of God at the close of the twentieth century, which is, to a significant extent, changing the shape of Protestant Christianity around the world. For almost 500 years Christian churches have largely functioned within traditional denominational structures of one kind or another. Particularly in the 1990s, but with roots going back for almost a century, new forms and operational procedures began to emerge in areas such as local church government, interchurch relationships, financing, evangelism, missions, prayer, leadership selection and training, the role of supernatural power, worship and other important aspects of church life. Some of these changes are being seen within denominations themselves, but for the most part they are taking the form of loosely structured apostolic networks. In virtually every region of the world, these new apostolic churches constitute the fastest growing segment of Christianity.[10]

Many in the Church today believe that a so-called "new apostolic paradigm" is necessary in order for it to break through the barriers of unbelief in our world. This proposed transformation has, at its core, a presupposition that the existing Church must move from "an audience into an army." While preparing for a Doctor of Ministry course in July 1998, I read the book *Church for the Unchurched* by George G. Hunter III. In this book, Hunter describes the kind of congregations that are needed today.

> Another growing church stresses that the people are the ministers and the pastors are the administrators. The pastor explains it this way, 'The staff make most of the necessary administrative decisions, thus freeing the laity from the consuming involvements that immobilize, divide, and exhaust most congregations, thereby freeing the people's time and energy for ministry and outreach in the community.' The goal for that church is to turn an audience into an army. ...Jesus did not tell the world to go to church. He told the church to go to the world.[11]

Since 1980, Wagner and others began to expand established church growth principles to include what he calls "spiritual dimensions."[12] As this expansion progressed, Wagner experienced a personal Pentecost and adopted a theological position that proposed aggressive "warfare prayer."[13]

> What we have discovered, however, is that all the evangelistic technology in the world will have only a minimal effect unless the spiritual battle is won. It is like a brand new automobile with all the latest engineering. It may be beautiful and perfectly constructed, but it will do nothing until gasoline is pumped into the tank. The same thing applies to spiritual power in evangelism and church growth.

> To illustrate, look at the decade of the 1980s in America. This was a decade of the mushrooming of some of the largest churches the nation has ever seen. Almost every metropolitan area now has one or more megachurches it did not have previously. Church growth seminars and evangelistic resources have multiplied. Private Christian schools and the Christian use of the media increased dramatically. On the surface it looked like Christianity was making great progress in the

nation. But statistics paint another picture. At the end of the decade church attendance was the same as at the beginning, and Protestant church membership had decreased. I believe God wants us to do a better job of evangelizing our nation in the years to come. And we will do it, in my opinion to the degree we understand that the real battle is spiritual.[14]

Wagner recounts two discoveries that revolutionized his understanding of church growth. During the Lausanne II Congress on World Evangelization, he formally challenged participants to consider two truths. First, "evangelism would work better when accompanied by serious prayer." Secondly, "throughout the Body of Christ, God had gifted, called and anointed certain individuals who were unusually powerful in the ministry of intercession."[15]

The outworking of these concepts during the '90s became for Wagner a monumentally important period. He states, "I sense, along with many other Christian leaders, that the Holy Spirit is saying, 'Prepare for warfare.' This decade may see the most intense spiritual warfare of recent times."[16]

A so-called "Spiritual Warfare Network" was formed to provide the necessary leadership in advancing this new apostolic reformation. In an article published by Wagner's "Global Harvest Ministries," Chuck Pierce recounts a dream he had summarizing the conceptual linkage between warfare intercession and the new apostolic paradigm:

> Recently I awakened with this phrase going over and over in my heart: "Strategic, prophetic intercession must be properly aligned with apostolic government for spiritual breakthrough and harvest of a region to occur." I saw that if intercessors entered into a new level of praying, and connected with apostolic authority within regions, the Lord would have dominion over the harvest fields of the earth. Dominion is a good word to understand. This word has been abused and misused so many times that I feel it is necessary for us to review. Without understanding the word dominion, we can never take apostolic authority of a region. Dominion

means the power to rule which forces a territory to recognize and subject itself to an authority or government. Even though dominion and authority can be greatly abused, there is an incredible principle throughout the Word of God concerning boundaries, dominion, and authority.[17]

It is this enlarged emphasis on apostles that even for some traditional charismatic churches and denominations has caused concern and vigorous disagreement. In August 2000, the General Council of the American Assemblies of God issued a statement calling new apostolic teachings "deviant."[18] The Church has increased its scrutiny. An important focus for the debate has been arriving at a precise definition of the word *apostle*. Wagner is careful to define his terms but also pointedly excludes three characteristics that many consider essential.

> An apostle is a Christian leader gifted, taught, commissioned, and sent by God with the authority to establish the foundational government of the church within an assigned sphere of ministry by hearing what the Spirit is saying to the churches and by setting things in order accordingly for the growth and maturity of the church.

> What I have excluded in this definition: There are three biblical characteristics of apostles which some include in their definition of apostle, but which I have chosen not to include: (1) signs and wonders (2 Cor. 12:12), (2) seeing Jesus personally (1 Cor. 9:1), and (3) planting churches (1 Cor. 3:10). My reason for this is that I do not understand these three qualities to be non-negotiables. They characterize many, perhaps most, apostles. But if a given individual lacks the anointing for one or more of them, this, in my opinion, would not exclude that individual from being a legitimate apostle.[19]

Wagner is expanding on the traditional understanding of apostolic ministries by including the modern-day necessity of adding other people who have giftedness in order to "unlock" regions of the earth that are resistant to the Gospel. Global Harvest Ministries (GHM) and the Spiritual Warfare Network (SWN) have made a decision based on spiritual revelation. It is also based on pure pragmatism. The emphasis on "apostolic leadership" is intended to boost the Church's evangelistic effectiveness and governmental efficiency. On GHM's website, an organization called the "International Coalition of Apostles" is described:

> Given the worldwide multiplication of individuals recognized by other Christian leaders as apostles, a strong desire has been expressed by many of them to be able to relate, in some structured way, to peer-level apostles in their own nations and internationally. Since autonomy is a high value for members of differing apostolic networks, the apostolic leaders of these networks, who technically are "vertical" apostles, had little access to mechanisms designed to fulfill that lingering "horizontal" desire to meet with their peers in anything other than a casual way.

> The International Coalition of Apostles was organized as one attempt to meet this need. It is not an exclusive organization since other similar groups are forming in different parts of the world, much to the delight of ICA, as a response to what the Spirit currently seems to be saying to the churches of the 21st Century.[20]

It is apparent to me that ICA's essential function is in military language, command, and control. (C2) The SWN, through its World Prayer Center in Colorado Springs, is attempting to achieve world situational awareness. Effective C2 is absolutely essential to any combat operation. The World Prayer Center's staff, with their impressive array of computer technology and list of intercessors, is able to bring a spiritual artillery barrage on any target in the world! Decisive spiritual force is celebrated and elicited by the SWN in order to loose Satan's hold on a person, situation, or geographical territory. Since Satan engages the Church with decisive spiritual force, the Church must also engage Satan with various levels of strategic and ground level warfare. To conduct successful "military" operations, the SWN needed to completely transform its purpose, structure, communications, strategy, and tactics. In short, it needed to instill in the Church a spiritual warrior ethos. The parallels between that what the United States Army is doing today are striking!

The Army Transformation program is all-encompassing. It seeks to rewrite out-of-date "doctrinal" statements that field an Objective Force projected to be relevant to the year 2020. Not only must high-priced weapon systems like the "Stryker" vehicles be fielded, but the ultimate weapon system, the "soldier," must be completely refitted and re-indoctrinated. Perhaps what the SWN desires to develop in the spiritual realm is the equivalent of the Army's new "Stryker Brigades." It is conceivable that the advocates of this highly mobile spiritual warfare army are attempting to bring decisive spiritual force to bear with Christian soldiers that can physically travel to hotspots anywhere in the world or be deployed with prayer at a moment's notice. To do so, they are well on their way in organizing relationships between "apostles" and intercessors. Spiritual C2 is being refined between what the author equates with U.S. Army theater Commanders in Chiefs or (CINCs) and the tactical commanders and troops on the ground. Wagner outlines the importance of this connection in his article "Apostles and Intercessors."[21]

> We didn't really understand this during the time that we were praying for the 10/40 Window in the 1990's. Now, however, as we are praying for the 40/70 Window, we are readjusting our strategy so that we do everything possible to connect apostles with intercessors. Our current desire is to launch at least one prayer journey into each of the 64 nations of the 40/70 Window every year until 2005. The intercessors doing these prayer journeys will only reach their full potential if they connect personally with apostles in each nation or region. This is essential because intercessors do not have the governmental authority, both in the visible world and in the invisible world that apostles do. The gift and office of intercessor began to be recognized widely in the 1970's, and

it has been growing ever since. As a result of our concentrated efforts over the past 12 years, a critical mass of high-level prophetic intercessors has now been identified and mobilized. However, this is not yet true of apostles, largely because the gift and office of apostle was not widely recognized until well into the 1990s. But the apostolic movement is developing rapidly.[22]

It is interesting to note that this movement is still emerging. There is no unified understanding or consensus on the role of apostles and their interplay with "prophetic intercessors." Although various apostolic summits are being held around the world, the European Summit in Oslo, Norway, in May of 2002 highlighted the evolution of the theological concepts. Wagner describes efforts to identify and mobilize apostles:

Thirty-seven apostles attended, representing 17 nations of Europe plus 3 nations outside of Europe (U.S.A., Singapore, and Kazakhstan). Some of them understood the theory and practice of apostolic ministry well before they came, but for others it was still a new and untested concept.[23]

The Need for a Spiritual Warrior Ethos

If the Church is at war, aggressive spiritual warriors are needed. A particular kind of combatant must be recruited and trained in order to conduct effective offensive and defensive operations. God requires people who sincerely want to be warriors. What kind of war are they fighting? In *Wrestling with Dark Angels,* the co-authors state, "We are all to be involved in spiritual warfare on at least three levels. First, there is the objective level, reaching unbelievers with the gospel. Next is the subjective level, protecting ourselves and our families from succumbing to the demonic warfare directed against us. Finally, there is the Christian level, helping to free demonized Christians from demonization."[24]

Advocates of the spiritual warfare movement assert that the Church needs soldiers who are seriously committed to personal combat with Satan and his demonic hordes. In effect, a warrior ethos must be cultivated and sustained that convinces ordinary parishioners as well as church leadership that "watchmen" are desired. It will be remembered that soldiers of the United States are required as a part of their initial "soldierization" training to memorize and obey the General Orders of the Army. One of the most important orders is "to guard their post until properly relieved."

For Old Testament Israel, the role of the watchman is well established. Hosea, the prophet, dreaded the imminent judgment of God. In his prophecy, he states, "The days of punishment have come, the days of retribution have come; Let Israel know this! The prophet is a fool, the inspired man is demented, because of the grossness of your iniquity, and because your hostility is so great. Ephraim was a watchman with my God, a prophet; yet the snare of a bird catcher is in all his ways, and there is only hostility in the house of God." (Hosea 9:7-8, NIV) James Boice, in his expositional commentary, *The Minor Prophets*, comments on the high-stakes game Israel was playing. In this case, the watchman is to be equated with the prophet.

> It is a grim picture. But it is not as grim as it was soon to become, for the very reason that the word of God was at least still being spoken at that point in Israel's history. The prophets might be laughed at. Their word might be disregarded. But as long as the prophets were there (whether they were respected or not), as long as the word of God was spoken (whether it was listened to or not), as long as those things were present there was hope.[25]

In Ezekiel, we again find numerous references to a watchman. In chapter 33:7, we read, "Now as for you, son of man, I have appointed you a watchman for the house of Israel; so you will hear a message from My mouth, and give them warning from Me." (NIV) What an awesome task it was to be appointed by God as His watchman!

> First a general principle is stated. The setting of watchmen to watch for the enemy was a common occurrence. Every

border would have its watchtowers, every city its watchmen. And, as soon as an enemy was seen to be approaching, the long curved horns the watchmen carried would be sounded as a warning to the people, and would go on being sounded until they were sure that the people had heard. This gave those in the fields the opportunity to flee within the walled cities for refuge, and enabled the defending troops to ready themselves.

The responsibility was a great one, and they would use men with sharp eyes. The safety of the people would depend on their early warning. But once they had given their warning their task was done. It was then up to others to take notice of the warning and implement what was necessary for deliverance, and for those in the fields to seek refuge. Any failure then would not be the responsibility of the watchman, but of those who heard the warning.

But if the watchman saw the enemy coming and did not give warning, then their blood would rest on him. He would have failed in his duty and would be to blame for all that followed. It was an awesome responsibility. They would be blood guilty in the eyes of the relatives of the dead, and in the eyes of God.[26]

The word translated as "watchman" in both texts is rendered in the Septuagint as *scopos*. According to Kittel's *Theological Dictionary of the New Testament,* "the word is attested from Homer in two senses: (a) it denotes one who directs a watchful glance on something, e.g., as an overseer...also a spy. The most common use from Homer's Iliad, 2, 792 is the military one for the guard, spy or scout. (b) *scopos* means the 'mark' e.g., of shooting...which one may hit or miss...Thus man has a goal which controls his whole life..."[27] It is also interesting to note that the word *scopos* and its corresponding forms are found in Attic. The meaning is "to look at," especially "to look at critically as the judge does."[28] In the New Testament, the term *scopein* occurs only in Luke 11:35 and Philippians 3:17. These usages "remind us of the sense 'to consider something critically and then hold something before one as a model on the basis of the inspection'."[29] The original Hebrew meaning "means to look about, to view from a distance. The primary idea is that of inclining or bending forward in order to behold...a watchman stationed on a tower."[30]

The warfare intercessors of the SWN, during their spiritual mapping of geographical areas of the world, are clearly more than casual observers of the world's scene. The prayer journeys they take at their own expense are solely for the purpose of critically observing and judging demonic "high-places." SWN's "high-level" intercessors are scouting out spiritual pressure points for the purpose of bringing Satanic strongholds to naught. Here is an example from February 12, 2004, that made headline news. There can be no question that the issue of same-sex marriage and the entire homosexual agenda is threatening the nation. Through the strategic prayer intercessors, a mighty avalanche of spiritual power can be unleashed. Chuck Pierce, vice-president of Global Harvest Ministries writes:

> I believe we are all closely watching the ongoing debate occurring in Massachusetts over the legality of same sex marriage. There is no coincidence that our USSPN Weekly State Prayer Focus is for Massachusetts this week. Sandy Heacock, our USSPN Regional Coordinator for New England and resident of that state, wrote me early this morning requesting our prayers at this key time. Her request appears below. Cindy Jacobs has also shared her concern that the Massachusetts Supreme Court decision to approve same sex marriage is opening a "door" in our nation that could unleash great harm in various areas. I would encourage you to pray fervently regarding this issue, and declare that the Lord's covenant relationship of marriage between one man and one woman would be protected in our nation.[31]

Another amazing example from the international realm is also incredible because it specifically speaks about the importance of "watching."

Yesterday morning (Feb. 11th) a worship *watch* (Italics mine) was in progress at a location just south of the Old City of Jerusalem. These watches are part of "Succat Hallel" a worship ministry in Jerusalem (of which the writers are a part) in which believers both from Israel and the Nations gather regularly to minister to the Lord in praise, worship and intercession. At 10:15 our friend Rick Ridings was reading aloud Psalm 99, which begins, "THE LORD REIGNS, LET THE PEOPLE TREMBLE; HE IS ENTHRONED ABOVE THE CHERUBIM, LET THE EARTH SHAKE! THE LORD IS GREAT IN ZION . . ." Precisely at the moment he finished the psalm, the room began to tremble. In fact this whole area of the Middle East began to shake as a 5-point earthquake rumbled through Israel. Centered at the north end of the Dead Sea, it was felt throughout Israel "from Dan to Beer Sheba" and extended beyond as far north as Beirut, Lebanon and Syria, and westward to Amman, Jordan. In Jerusalem the quake lasted only about 20 seconds, but veterans with whom we have spoken don't remember one which felt so strong. In God's mercies, no one was killed in the quake and there was little damage to structures. Experts say that if it had been one point higher, the damage would likely have been extremely severe. Significantly, in this same Worship Watch, even as Psalm 99 was being read, another worshipper in the room already had her Bible opened preparing to share from Revelation 11:13, which speaks of a future earthquake in Jerusalem in which 1/10 of the city will fall...[32]

The principal battle focus of the SWN is to pull down the strongholds of Satan so that the unimpeded Gospel may envelop the hearts of those who do not yet believe. One cannot discuss combat leadership in a spiritual context unless the experience and example of Joshua is highlighted. A divine pattern for his entire campaign to conquer the Promised Land is found in his assault of the city of Jericho. When he was given the mantle of leadership of Israel, he also became a CINC over all the armies. One of Joshua's main challenges was to instill a warrior ethos in a population that had previously been stigmatized as slaves. Highlighting Joshua's ancestry, Richard D. Nelson's Old Testament Library's *Joshua* pays special attention to his warrior training and identity. W. Phillip Keller says, "I Chronicles 7:27 provides Joshua with an Ephraimite geneaology... As an Ephraimite hero, he may have been most originally at home in the Divine Warrior narrative centered on Ephramite Beth-horon (Joshua 10:10-14)."[33] Combined with his soldier-heart, Joshua also was a man of keen spiritual insight. He understood that the real contest was between God and man. Referring to the golden calf incident at the foot of Mount Sinai, W. Phillip Keller comments about what Joshua saw and felt:

> Better than his elder, (Moses), Joshua immediately grasped the enormity of the evil precipitated by the perverse people caught up in their idol worship. With remarkable sensitivity to the titanic spiritual struggle now under way Joshua knew there was war between man and God. The superficial singing, the strident shouting, the horrible dances were but a front, a facade to mask the flagrant effrontery to God Almighty.[34]

Not only was Joshua able to articulate feelings and spiritual truth, he was also able to communicate and lead an often intransigent people. Nelson again states, "As his name seems to signify (Sir. 46:1), Joshua was the ideal 'savior,' who not only won battles and secured possession of the land, but was able to hold the people to perfect loyalty his whole life." (Joshua 24:31)[35]

In the final analysis, spiritual leaders need to hear from God before they can lead the people of God. Joshua remembered Moses choosing him to travel to Sinai. For all his life, he would revert back to that incredible event at the burning bush. Preparing to attack the seemingly impregnable fortress of Jericho, he once again hears from God:

> ...From the camp of Gilgal he "viewed the city." As yet no special direction had been given him how to attack Jericho, and, assuredly, the people whom he commanded were

untrained for such work. While such thoughts were busy within him, of a sudden, "as he lifted up his eyes and looked, there stood over against him," not the beleaguered city, but "a man with his sword drawn in his hand." Challenged by Joshua: "Art thou for us, or for our adversaries?" the strange warrior replied: "No! But I am the Captain (or Prince) of the host of Jehovah, now I am come." Here His speech was interrupted - for Joshua fell on his face before Him, and reverently inquired His commands. The reply: "Loose thy shoe from off thy foot, for the place whereon thou standest is holy," must have convinced Joshua that this Prince of the host of Jehovah was none other than the Angel of the Covenant, Who had spoken to Moses out of the burning bush (Exodus 3:4), and Who was co-equal with Jehovah...[36]

It is my opinion that the SWN is feverishly trying to establish a new warrior ethos for the entire Protestant Church. During the last twelve years, Peter Wagner and a growing list of others have been systematically creating spiritual battle plans and operating structures that do much more than shift the church growth paradigm. There is considerable evidence that GHM and other spin-off organizations are fundamentally altering traditional church growth theory and practice. The establishment of numerous categories and "spheres" of apostles and intercessors presents the evidence. At one point, Wagner describes two major "apostolic" categories with four or five sub-categories. He admittedly uses a "phenomenological" approach to leadership.

Among practicing apostles, I have found a relatively low level of practical understanding of apostolic spheres. All apostles recognize that they have divine authority, but not all are aware that this authority is only activated within a divinely appointed sphere. Once apostles get outside of their sphere, they have no more authority than any other member of the body of Christ...

The current apostolic movement is so new, and it is developing at such a dizzying speed, that a considerable amount of confusion has arisen. Who is an apostle? Are all apostles the same? How do bona fide apostles minister? I believe that the answers to these and other similar questions will emerge through a phenomenological approach. This is the methodology that I have used to arrive at a continually developing set of conclusions. Terminology that accurately describes current apostolic phenomena will greatly help dispel the confusion.[37]

Listed below are the various categories of apostolic ministry. Because the approach is "phenomenological", presumably the groupings and the descriptions are subject to change. The categories as of 16 March 2001 are:

Vertical Apostles:

1. Ecclesiastical apostles. Apostles who are given authority over a sphere which includes a number of churches, presumably in an apostolic network headed up by the apostle.
2. Functional apostles. Apostles who are given authority over those who have an ongoing ministry in a certain specific sphere of service which has defined boundaries of participation.
3. Apostolic Team Members. Apostles whose apostolic ministry functions in conjunction with an apostle who is seen as the leader of a team of one or more other peer-level vertical apostles. They may be assigned specific spheres by the leading apostle. These are more than administrators or assistants or armor-bearers.
4. Congregational apostles. Apostles functioning as senior pastors of dynamic, growing churches of more than 700-800.

Horizontal Apostles:

1. Convening apostles. Apostles who have authority to call together on a regular basis peer-level leaders who minister in a defined field.
2. Ambassadorial apostles. Apostles who have itinerant, frequently international, ministries of catalyzing and nurturing apostolic movements on a broad scale.
3. Mobilizing apostles. Apostles who have the authority to take leadership in bringing together qualified leaders in the body of Christ for a specific cause or project.
4. Territorial apostles. Apostles who have been given authority for leading a certain segment of the body of Christ in a given territorial sphere such as a city or state.
5. Marketplace Apostles. It seems clear that some marketplace apostles would be vertical (perhaps within a large company) while others would be horizontal (bringing together peer-level marketplace apostles). The more we work with marketplace apostles, the more clarity will come in due time.

Note: Dr. Wagner functions as a horizontal apostle within a sphere of recognized apostles. As such, Dr. Wagner does not provide apostolic 'covering' or accountability as a vertical apostle.[38]

It has been stated before that the SWN has discovered that when intercessors are "connected" with apostles, more spiritual power is released. In 1992, Peter Wagner wrote the book *Prayer Shield*. In his book, Wagner separates personal intercessors into three groups. "He observes that intercessors operate in three concentric circles around the leader. 1. The inner circle: Here we picture the pastor along with what I will call I-1 intercessors, 2. The middle circle: This contains I-2 intercessors, and 3. The outer circle: This contains I-3 intercessors... Think of I-1 intercessors as having a close personal relationship to the pastor, the I-2 intercessors as having a casual relationship, and the I-3 intercessors as having a remote relationship to the pastor."[39] Wagner believes that not all intercessors have the spiritual gift of intercession. The unmistakable result is these inter-cessors are "watchmen" in their own right when it comes to doing spiritual combat.

A helpful analysis of what happens spiritually in situa-tions like this comes from Sylvia R. Evans of Elim Bible Fellowship in Lima, New York. She says that one of God's most wonderful blessings is His faithfulness 'to waken inter-cessors for the 'night watch' or an 'early morning watch' and to place them on duty to hold off the enemy.' She sees inter-cessors as watchmen constantly on the alert to be assigned their position in battle.

Speaking of the full armor of God in Ephesians 6, Evans interprets the passage as suggesting that the intercessor 'is to be able to aggressively withstand the enemy, taking the attack for others who may be the real target. The watchman must be able to quench all the fiery darts, not only against himself or herself but also against the ones for whom they are standing watch.'[40]

The proponents of this aggressive prayer warfare use interces-sion as their primary weapon. It is this writer's experience that many Protestant Christians use prayer with a kind of "sugar-daddy" approach. Believers, whether they are in fellowship with God or their neighbor, mistakenly appropriate prayer selfishly. We as human beings are, in fact, essentially egocentric with motives that are often hopelessly mixed. Perhaps the greatest contribution the spiritual warfare movement makes to the Church's understanding and practice of prayer is its reexamination of the essence of intercession. What is intercession? The Global Harvest Ministries fervently desire that the Church get intercession correct. GHM states, "We often use the word 'intercession' as a synonym for 'prayer.' Though in a general sense, this is an acceptable practice, it is not technically correct. Intercession is coming to God on behalf of another. All intercession is prayer, but all prayer is not intercession! 'Intercession' is derived from the Latin '*inter,*' meaning 'between' and *cedere,* meaning 'to go.' Intercession, then, is going between or standing in the gap." (See Ezekiel 22:30)[41]

Matthew Henry's *Commentary of the Whole Bible* says:

> There is a way of standing in the gap, and making up the breach against the judgments of God, by repentance, and prayer, and reformation. Moses stood in the gap when he made intercession for Israel to turn away the wrath of God, (Psalm 106:23). When God is coming forth against a sinful people to destroy them *he expects some to intercede for them,* (Italics mine) and enquires if there be but one that does; so much is it his desire and delight to show mercy. If there be but a man that stands in the gap, as Abraham for Sodom, he will discover him and be well pleased with him.[42]

The spiritual warfare movement is showing great leadership by re-emphasizing for the Church a commitment to cultivate Christian warriors who "stand in the gap" around the world. The new apostolic reformation is rapidly rewriting established methodologies in church growth so that God's great mercy will rain down upon pagan peoples who will perish in their sins without watchmen to fend off the enemy of their souls.

The grand theme of waging spiritual warfare is not new to the Church. The author believes that this warfare is indeed on multiple levels. It is helpful to reflect on the work of an ancient Christian poet from Hispania. Aurelius Prudentius Clemens lived in the northeast province of Tarraconensis, modern Calahorra in A.D. 348.[43] He was a layman who wrote not for liturgical purposes, but rather for a believers' personal devotional life. Robert Wilken states, "He composed the first Christian epic, a long, allegorical poem called *Psychomachia* whose title is best translated 'spiritual warfare.'"[44]

> The poem is about the inner life, about the struggle within us to set free the 'heart that is enslaved', a battle that is waged over who or what should rule our lives. In a phrase that has distinctly Augustinian overtones, Prudentius says

that 'human nature is divided. (The poem) is about how to rid ourselves of double-mindedness and attain purity of heart.[45]

Prudentius was dedicated in preparing a poetic training manual for spiritual warfare. He correctly perceived that Christians urgently needed practical, leader-driven "Individual Entry Training." The warrior-king David knew how important training was. He said, "Blessed be the Lord, my rock, who trains my hands for war, and my fingers for battle..." (Psalm 144:1, RSV).

PART IV: TRAINING THE FORCE

CHAPTER SIX

THE TRAINING AND DOCTRINE COMMAND OF THE U.S. ARMY

The Needs of the Army

Training has always been an integral part of all the Army is or does. To understand the essence of "training," it is instructive to discover exactly what the Psalmist meant by the concept of training a soldier force. The LXX's term for the word "train" in Psalm 144:1 and one hundred other places in the Old Testament is *didaskein*. To the Greek-speaking Jews, this term came to have a more technical significance. Kittel's *Theological Dictionary of the New Testament* states that *didaskein* "always lays claim to the whole man and not merely to certain parts of him."[1] The United States Army's transformation of civilians into soldiers involves a complete attitudinal, physical, and technical reorientation. Indeed, "training" soldiers must encompass the whole person!

The "Bible" for training the Army is the Training and Doctrine Commands' regulation 350-6. This very extensive document covers every imaginable facet of a new recruit's life. The Army needs

TRADOC to be the watchdog over Army standards. If the training standards wane or fail to adapt to the needs of changing threats, soldiers will die. The goal of what is called "soldierization" is contained in the regulation.

> The goal of IET is to transform civilians into technically and tactically competent soldiers who live by the Army's values and are prepared to take their place in the ranks of the Army. This transformation from civilian to soldier is accomplished during a five-phased "soldierization" process which begins with a soldier's arrival at the reception battalion and ends with the awarding of a MOS upon completion of IET. By definition, soldierization is a tough, comprehensive process which totally immerses a IET soldier in a positive environment established by active, involved leadership. This environment sets high standards, provides positive role models, and uses every training opportunity to reinforce basic soldier skills. This demands that all soldiers in IET, regardless of rank, strictly adhere to the standards of excellence and commitment that set the United States Army apart from others and make it the world's best professional army.

> It is essential that the officers and non-commissioned officers (NCOs) and Department of the Army (DA) civilians assigned the crucial responsibility of transforming America's sons and daughters into professional soldiers be motivated, disciplined, and competent professionals.[2]

The Army, especially during the Global War on Terror, needs soldiers who are totally immersed into the warrior ethos previously described. To make sure America develops the warriors she needs, TRADOC must during these first five phases of IET training concentrate on inculcating the well-known Army slogan, "train as you fight." A former Sergeant Major of the Army named Glen E. Morrell says, "We must train in peacetime because there is not time in war...Well-qualified soldiers, physically and mentally toughened by hard-training, led by competent and caring leaders and dedicated to preserving the values they and their fellow countrymen live by, make the critical difference between a successful and unsuccessful Army."[3] This kind of emphasis is called by the Army "battle-focused training." Army Field Manual 25-101 states, "Battle focus is a concept used to derive peacetime training requirements from wartime missions. Units cannot achieve and sustain proficiency on all possible soldier, leader, and collective tasks. Commanders must selectively identify and train on those tasks that accomplish the unit's critical wartime mission..."[4]

Like all large organizations, armies change. The Army must change its training approach as a result of the "War on Terror." Changing any large institution is never easy. I have mentioned before that the new Chief of Staff of the Army, General Peter J. Schoomaker, is reconfiguring what all soldiers must learn and sustain in their assigned units, regardless of MOS. On February 1, 2004, the Army Chief of Ordnance at APG, Brigadier General Michael Lenaers, wrote an e-mail note to his Command Sergeant Major, Anthony T. Aubain. In this note, BG Lenaers informed his top enlisted NCO that sweeping changes to IET training were possible. My former brigade commander, Colonel Paul Meredith sent me a copy of the proposed IET training changes and commented, "Many decisions to be made, but you can see what direction they are headed. We are certainly in for some major changes. Out-of-the-box thinking going on."[5] The "changes" COL Meredith referred to are described in a PowerPoint presentation entitled "Initial Entry Training for An Army At War," given to Lieutenant General Cavin, Deputy Commanding General of TRADOC on 30 January, 2004.[6] In this briefing on "proposed" changes to IET training, the focus centers on renewed attention on what is called "combatives" and addresses the immediate needs of an army at war! The briefing describes a change of "focus of IET culture, program of instruction (POI) and methodology." The Army is beginning to shift away from a more benign training approach to a more aggressive warrior mentality. The proposed objectives for this new approach to IET training are:

From graduating a soldier ready to join a unit, to graduating soldiers ready to win and survive in combat; From

garrison to field; From drill and ceremony to tactical movements and combat drills; From passing the Army Physical
Fitness Test (APFT) to campaign endurance, combat fitness
and combatives; From qualification on the M16 rifle to
employment of weapons found in today's units; From soldierization and Army values to soldierization, Army values and
the Warrior Ethos.[7]

These so-called "combatives" will be skills required to grad-
uate from Basic Combat Training (BCT). They will include hand-
to-hand combat, a complete bayonet assault course, field-survival
knowledge with advanced first aid, battle drills, more emphasis on
land navigation and hand grenades, and qualification on a rigorous
nuclear-biological-chemical (NBC) course.[8] It is not that these skills
were totally absent from BCT, but now, the classes will be greatly
expanded and the training will be more rigorous. It remains to be
seen exactly how the new BCT and Advanced Individual Training
(AIT) courses will be configured. At a minimum, the training will
move soldiers from "apprentice soldier to warrior soldier."[9]

The Philosophies of Basic and Advanced Individual Training

Although there will be some significant POI changes in the very
near future, the essential nature of IET training will remain. Civilians
in any army must be transformed into a fighting force. How does the
United States Army accomplish this task? What process of indoctri-
nation must be used to motivate an individual into a fighting team?
   The Army uses nine principles in training. These principles
according to FM 25-100 "provide direction, but are sufficiently
flexible to accommodate local conditions and the judgment of
commanders and other leaders."[10] The principles are: (1) Train as
a combined arms and service team, (2) Train as you fight, (3) Use
appropriate doctrine, (4) Use performance-oriented training, (5)
Train to challenge, (6) Train to sustain proficiency, (7) Train using
multi-echelon techniques, (8) Train to maintain, and (9) Make
commanders the primary trainers.[11]

Many years ago, when first entering the Army Reserve, I had an occasion with my young son, Mark, to visit the training post at Fort Dix, New Jersey. I was especially eager to have Mark view the reception center as new recruits stepped off the bus at BCT. We watched with fascination as hundreds of these would-be soldiers dropped their bags and formed ragged lines as their new drill sergeants barked orders. I wondered then how the Army would change these young men and women in the short weeks of basic training. The recruiting of civilians into the Army is serious business. A problem with the all-volunteer force is that recruiting now is all about marketing and money! An *Army Times* article in 1999 states, "Money, serious money, is at the center of a revamped campaign that features increased bonuses and new incentives for young people who enlist in the Army for two to six years...A single top-quality recruit could net $85,000 for enlisting in certain MOS's for four years..."[12] Training a recruit from start to finish could take another hundred thousand dollars. To make matters more serious, while at APG's training brigade, I was informed that about one-third of new soldiers do not complete the terms of even their first enlistment! These soldiers "wash" out for various physical and emotional reasons. Many new soldiers do not have the "right stuff."

It is the primary job of the drill sergeants (DS) to mold the recruit into a fully functioning soldier. More than anyone else, it is the NCO Corps that shapes the lives of America's sons and daughters. To perform the task of initial entry training, a DS must make various judgment calls that will literally determine whether a soldier stays or is discharged. Many of these soldiers are discharged within the first one hundred eighty days for "incompatibility." This discharge is non-prejudicial and is usually accomplished with administrative speed. A high percentage of these soldiers simply cannot take the mental discipline and physical demands of Army life. The problem is the Army is short of soldiers. It cannot afford to lose its time and money investment by releasing soldiers prematurely. Leaders are called upon to frequently make tough decisions about retention of IET soldiers. Often, a soldier will have trouble passing the physical fitness test or, because of medical or other personal appointments, may miss required training classes. The IET environment is one that is called the "Insist/Assist" philosophy.

Cadre will train their soldiers by building on and affirming their strengths and shoring up their weaknesses. It is imperative that unit cadre establish high standards of performance and insist their soldiers meet those standards. It then becomes incumbent on the cadre to coach, mentor, and assist their soldiers in meeting the standards through performance counseling and phase goal setting. This insist/assist philosophy must be balanced during implementation. Discharging potentially good soldiers merely because they fail to meet certain standards when additional coaching could bring them up to par is not in keeping with the intent of the soldierization process.

The leadership climate in IET must be positive. Leaders at all levels will demonstrate a genuine concern for the mission and the welfare of the individual soldier. Importance of the individual soldier to the Army and to the nation must be highlighted throughout the entire IET process.[13]

Throughout the IET process, soldiers are subjected to progressive and extended periods of stress. This is done so that the soldier will develop a capacity for combat scenarios. The training leadership seeks with coaching and mentoring atmospheres to create soldiers to be warriors. Each of the five phases of the IET training is designed to progressively apply mental and physical pressure. From the first "Patriot" phase that imposes total control over the recruit to the last phase that evaluates and awards the soldier's MOS, the Army seeks to produce soldiers who can survive and win in combat. However, the ante has now been raised because of the carnage of Operation Iraqi Freedom. The Army has recognized that they have "perhaps lost some of the edge associated with being a soldier."[14] Speaking on October 7, 2003 at the Association of the United States Army's annual meeting in Washington, DC, General Kevin Byrnes, Commander of the Army Training and Doctrine Command said the Army's training and education systems must change. He said the Army has "reinforced the culture where you're a technician first and a soldier second."[15] Lieutenant General William Wallace, Commander of the Combined Arms Center at Fort Leavenworth, Kansas said, "We're removing those impediments."

> To be a warrior, you've got to be able to use your individual weapon. You've got to be able to operate in small, lethal teams if called upon to do so. You've got to have that mental and physical capability to deal with the enemy regardless of whether you're a frontline soldier or you're someone fixing helicopters for a living, because you are a soldier first and a mechanic second.[16]

The Non-Commissioned Officer's Corps and Sergeant's Business

It has been said that "the backbone of the Army are sergeants." In more than twenty years of military service, I have concluded that this statement is true. The professional NCO is absolutely invaluable to the American Army. Sergeants at all levels are closest to the ordinary soldier. Although trained to obey the orders of officers, soldiers will first look to their section or platoon sergeant for guidance and direction. The motivational power of a good NCO is wonderful to see. The retired twelfth Sergeant Major of the Army (SMA), Jack L. Tilley, issued his "NCO Vision" that encapsulates what sergeants are meant to be. His vision was:

> An NCO Corps, grounded in heritage, values and tradition, that embodies the warrior ethos; values perpetual learning; and is capable of leading, training, and motivating soldiers...We must always be an NCO Corps that: leads by example, trains from experience, maintains and enforces standards, takes care of soldiers, and adapts to a changing world.[17]

The essence of "Sergeant's business" is training. The Army believes this maxim so much that once a week, normal day-to-day business completely stops for usually four to five hours for "Sergeant's Time." This period by commander's orders allows NCOs at all levels and MOS's to assess and engage in what is called "sustainment training" with their own section's soldiers. This time is sacred and no interruptions or "training distractors" are allowed. This practice originates from the Continental Army's woefully inadequate training state during the Revolutionary War. During the perilous time at Valley Forge, General George Washington persuaded a Prussian General named Frederick von Steuben to drill soldiers in rudimentary soldier skills. "(General) von Steuben gave the American Army life when it was nearing death at Valley Forge. One reason for the renewed life was the great care to the training and responsibilities of NCO's."[18]

The NCO trainers have an obligation to their soldiers to make the training interesting and relevant. The Army holds all of its leaders accountable to train soldiers according to what is called the Mission Essential Task List or (METL). The METL drives the content and, to some extent, the form of the training provided. The METL are those tasks that are deemed necessary for soldiers in a particular unit or section to perform during combat. This yearly emphasis may change as the Army reworks itself into a more lethal force. CSM Charles T. Tucker summarizes the NCO's task:

> All trainers have one objective: To develop the best possible soldier with the available time and resources. Obviously the emphasis is on developing a soldier's technical and leadership skills for combat. To develop these two skills, NCOs must concentrate primarily on the soldier's ability to successfully accomplish individual tasks. They must also teach their soldiers how important unit cohesion is for mission accomplishment. Individuals do not win wars; squads, platoons, and companies do.[19]

In 1982, I became an officer in the United States Army. Early in my career, I learned that while NCOs are the "backbone" of the Army, each officer by an Act of Congress is authorized to "command." This fact means that it is the officer who is ultimately held account-able for all that happens. Officers are the "head" that strengthens the "backbone."

The Officer Corps: Leading From the Front

When soldiers refer to an officer who "leads from the front," they offer a great compliment. An officer, also a non-commissioned officer, should be willing take career risks in order to properly train and advance the Army mission. The problem is, not many officers are risk-takers. The desire to protect one's career above all else seems to be an all-consuming pursuit. The experience of former Army Air Corps General, Billy Mitchell, during the pre-World War II era is certainly not the norm today. Mitchell was a visionary who fervently believed he could make the Army better. His aggressive pursuit of the so-called "Third Dimension" of warfare ultimately cost him his career and his rank. Court-martialed in 1925 for being too outspoken, he died a broken man. He gambled with his career and lost. A mere sixteen years later, the Japanese surprise air attack on Pearl Harbor would prove his prophecies correct.

At a time when young sailors were absorbing battle-ship doctrine at Annapolis and cadets were studying horse charges at West Point, Billy was convinced that airpower had radically changed warfare forever. Warriors accustomed to thinking in two dimensions—land and sea—now had to understand a "Third Dimension."

Not surprisingly, this was heresy to the traditionalists. Mitchell was a convincing speaker with a growing number of acolytes, but he was also an officer in the United States Army, subject to discipline. His superiors ordered him to tone it down. But when opposed, Billy only fought harder to convey his vision of the future. He took his case to the American people, because, as he often said, 'Changes in military systems come about only through the pressure of public opinion or disaster in war.'[20]

The issue of "change" for an institution like the Army has never been easy. Compounding the situation today is the perpetual problem of careerism. Most officers pride themselves on their leadership abilities. However, many officers are leaving the Army because of their perceptions that the Army, as an institution, simply does not listen. One officer, who has now retired after twenty years of service, describes his struggle thus:

>...The idea of serving beyond the 20-year mark became more and more questionable for me. The main reason for my personal doubt is the constantly changing culture in the Army which is becoming more concerned with producing a superficial image of accomplishment, guided by false caring vs. tackling our readiness issues with up-front leadership and firm solutions. The Army has become a "social experiment", geared towards promoting diversity and celebrating individual successes vs. instilling the sense of unity behind the values our constitution, the Flag and our distinguished unit colors. The end result we see today is clearly diminished combat readiness and a lower willingness by our young people to serve a higher cause...

>Senior Leaders are not listening. Listening, in our Army, is a lost art. The attitude of "father knows best" will definitely not lead to major changes in our current situation of eroding combat readiness and rapidly disappearing benefits. One should always remember that the most significant changes in military affairs were not the result of General Officer initiatives but were initiated by junior and mid-grade officers who, in many cases, put their future and careers at risk.[21]

My personal experience of nineteen years of active duty dovetails with Lieutenant Colonel Zimmerman. The "lead from the front"

Army ideal has been politically "elbowed out" by a philosophy of leadership that is more concerned about being promoted than doing the right thing. Unless the Army begins to reward out-of-the-box thinking, leaders at the mid-grade ranks and junior leaders will not invest twenty years in an Army career. The Army's leadership is eroding. Any organization's future lies with its junior leadership. In the Army, junior leaders are severely disappointed and they are, therefore, voting with their feet.

Concerns about Junior Leaders

My interest in the Army's junior leadership became personal in February 2003. While Second Lieutenant (2LT) Alan R. Fowler was enrolled in APG's Officer Basic Course (OBC), he met and married my daughter Melissa. Alan was a former enlisted man who was chosen for the Army's Green to Gold program. Taking an enlisted person and making him wear the gold bar of a second lieutenant made my son-in-law really internalize some valuable insights. His experiences at OBC provided me with a window into what is happening with the Army's junior leaders. During this army school, 2LT Fowler shared with me his perceptions. For the most part, he believed the course was superficial in content and arbitrary in its grading and evaluation procedures. My interpretation of his comments led me to believe that the Army has a serious cultural problem with these "Generation X-ers." There is a wide emotional and attitudinal divide between today's Army Lieutenants and Captains.

Dr. Leonard Wong, of the United States Army War College Strategic Studies Institute recently released a monograph entitled "Generations Apart: X-ers and Boomers in the Officer Corps." It is an excellent look at the junior officer retention challenge as a symptom of an internal cultural clash between junior officers (Generation X—or X-ers) and senior officers (Baby Boomers—or just "Boomers"), instead of simply the result of external forces such as OPTEMPO and a booming economy. This work is significant, because if Army policy makers take the time to read and understand it, they may begin to comprehend fully the message that junior officers are trying to send. These are job satisfaction concerns centered on deep-seated Army cultural issues. Too often lately, we see attempts to control the junior officer exodus through targeted measures such as pay raises, more days off, and now, email access to senior officers. These measures are perks—they are not true solutions because they deal with the symptoms instead of the cause.[22]

In reality, there is a "trust deficit" between "Boomer" senior officers and the "Gen X" junior officers. While at APG as training brigade chaplain, I had numerous occasions to hear and observe both generational perceptions and complaints. The bottom line seems to focus on the role of relationships and loyalty in the Army. Loyalty, after all, is one of the Army's seven core values. These two groups of officers simply understand loyalty differently.

Dr. Wong makes the statement that X-er loyalty is "based on a bond of trust between the Army and the officer." Is this really a difference between generations? Does he really mean to imply that Boomer officers base loyalty on something other than a bond of trust? Are senior officers reading his monograph and slapping their foreheads, saying, "Ohhhh. Trust. Jeez. Crazy kids." I cannot believe this is a revelation; I'd like to think both generations view loyalty the same way...

Xers are realists. The needs of the Army come first. We understand that, but perhaps the difference is that we really do hold the Army to its "Be All You Can Be" promise. We see it as a mutual contract: I'll give it 100%, and the Army in turn will provide me the opportunity to reach my full potential.[23]

What has happened to the Army, whose slogan a few short years ago was "Be All You Can Be?" Without an understanding of the origins of the Army's present management philosophy, one cannot fully comprehend why so many junior leaders are disgruntled. The Army of today is viewed and run like a large modern corporation. Because this is so, the Army has a significant problem. The Army has too many Lieutenants and not enough Captains. As of 2002, the number of Captains leaving the Army had doubled over the last several years.[24] Junior officers are leaving the Army in droves.

There is a mismatch between input and output; namely the Captains are punching out faster than the required number of Lieutenants are getting promoted to Captain. The most frequent complaint made by the 'best and brightest' of our Captains as they depart is that they are fed up with being micromanaged to death in a zero defects, power-point driven culture that does not give them enough time in the field to learn the arts of soldiering, like troop command and tactical leadership.[25]

The Army's "solution" is akin to the proverbial "smoke and mirrors." Reducing the time-in-grade requirements for Lieutenants to only thirty-eight months instead of fifty-four severely deprives them of the necessary training and experience to be capable combat leaders. The Army's solution is a direct result of what is called "Ethical Egoism," predicated on the assumption that people "are motivated solely by self-interest."[26] After all, why wouldn't Lieutenants want to be promoted to Captain at the earliest possible time? This management theory was spawned by the Secretary of War, Elihu Root. He borrowed the management theories of Frederick Taylor during President William McKinley's administration in 1899. The Army, it was argued, was just another large corporation that needed an efficient "coercive pattern of dominance, subordinance and centralized control from the top."[27] By attempting to transform the Army into a leadership production line, Root and Taylor sought to devise a mechanistic process whereby soldiers were regarded as mere cogs in a wheel.

Enamored by the technology of the early 1900s, the Pentagon leadership is still haunted by a mechanistic personnel process more than one hundred years later. This time, it appears that many enlisted and junior officers are not willing to play the game. Desirous of reaching a true revolution in military affairs and its Objective Force, the Army Transformation program of the twenty-first century seems to be attempting to treat its soldiers in the personnel arena with mindless insensitivity. Because junior leaders are not robots but thrive on self-development and the mentoring relationships of superiors, the Army is short nineteen hundred captains.

Major Bob Krumm states an ominous warning: "While the senior Army leadership has risked the ire of politicians to push a new weapons system, it has been virtually silent about a crisis in the ranks that shows no signs of letting up. For most of a decade the Army has hemorrhaged young officers at an unsustainable rate. Should the exodus continue it matters less than ever what kind of weapons a transformed Army fields, because it won't have sufficient talent and experience to employ them."[28] The result may be a large number of prematurely promoted Captains who needlessly die in battle or make decisions that cost their soldiers' lives! Soldiers deserve to be informed and trained. Physical combat is costly. Officers are responsible for everything that happens or fails to happen.

> In a battlefield cemetery each marble cross marks an individual crucifixion. Someone, someone very young usually has died for somebody else's sins.

> The movie "Saving Private Ryan" begins and ends in the military cemetery above Omaha Beach. By sundown of D-Day, 40,000 Americans had landed on that beach, and one in 19 had become a casualty. The military brass purposely chose troops with no combat experience for the bulk of the assault force. The brass reasoned that an experienced infantryman is a terrified infantryman. The odds of dying in the early waves were so great that an informed soldier might be paralyzed with well-founded despair. But the young and idealistic might move forward into the lottery of death.[29]

This "lottery of death" is not restricted to the physical realm. Indeed, in the realm of the spirit, there is yet a more horrible and permanent death. Christian warriors must train strenuously and intelligently. It is important to remember the words of Jesus when He said, "And do not fear those who kill the body, but are unable to kill the soul; but rather fear him who is able to destroy both the soul and body in hell" (Matthew 10:28, NIV).

CHAPTER SEVEN

TRAINING DISCIPLES OF CHRIST

B asic training for military personnel is, of course, known as "boot camp." Soldiers are meticulously trained according to a prescribed "program of instruction," or POI. In the Army, there is very little deviation from a trainee's POI unless the particular exigencies of war and an enemy's tactics dictate the need for change. As previously mentioned, the United States Army is quickly adjusting its POI to address a particular set of war circumstances. With the adoption and implementation of a new "Warrior Ethos," the Army's BCT and AIT courses are stressing so-called "combatives." These warrior skills are designed to make the soldier more lethal and survivable on the twenty-first century battlefield. A new emphasis on skills focusing on hand-to-hand combat will enable the soldier to close with an enemy and emerge victorious. Everything is being designed to inculcate this "new" warrior ethos.

What defines a warrior? How does a person become a warrior? How can the Army ensure that all its Soldiers embody Warrior Ethos?

Those are questions the Army has attempted to answer for several years and has recently reached a solution.

Gen. Eric Shinseki, former chief of staff of the Army, directed (via a memorandum signed June 3, 2003) the development and implementation of a strategy that will ensure every Soldier understands and embodies true Warrior Ethos. Current Army Chief of Staff Gen. Peter Schoomaker re-emphasized Warrior Ethos, approving it in November 2003.

Recently Team Warrior, a division of <u>Task Force Soldier</u>, completed the development phase of a Warrior Ethos strategy and began implementing the plan, which is gaining attention Army-wide...

One way the team plans to instill Warrior Ethos is by creating a new standard for them to live by, which they outlined in the Soldiers' Creed—which Schoomaker approved Nov. 24. Schoomaker directed that the Soldier's Creed be disseminated Army-wide and taught to the force.[1]

There are many persons as advocates of the spiritual warfare movement who firmly believe that the Church needs to radically alter the training of believers and develop a spiritual warrior ethos. Perhaps it is time for the Church also to adopt and implement a "Christian Soldier's Creed." For the Church to take spiritual combat seriously, training in "spiritual combatives" is necessary. When should a disciple take spiritual basic training? What should be included in a local church's POI? Who should conduct the training? Obviously each denomination and local congregation should decide these issues. All training is designed to accomplish the mission. In the military, one always starts with the mission. What is the "mission" that Christian soldiers should be trained to accomplish? A soldier is trained to accomplish a mission and then is deemed "mission capable." Are the majority of people who name the name of Christ mission capable?

You were made for a mission. God is at work in the world, and he wants you to join him. This assignment is called your *mission*. God wants you to have both a ministry in the

Body of Christ and a mission in the world. Your ministry is your service to *believers,* and your mission is your service to *unbelievers...* Our English word *mission* comes from the Latin word for "sending." Being a Christian includes being *sent* into the world as a representative of Jesus Christ. Jesus said, *'As the Father has sent me, I am sending you.'* (John 20:21, NIV)... The mission Jesus had while on earth is now *our* mission because we are the Body of Christ...What is that mission? Introducing people to God!... *'Christ changed us from enemies into his friends and gave us the task of making others his friends also.'* (2 Corinthians 5:18, TEV)... Fulfilling your life mission on earth is an essential part of living for God's glory.[2]

Any army unit or section before engaging in combat training must first identify its "mission essential task list," or METL. The METL drives everything an army unit does. In accomplishing the mission "tasks," the Army differentiates between *stated* and *implied* tasks. The commander must state what he or she wants accomplished, and then it is up to the staff to identify and carry out these tasks. One could say these tasks become the objectives to reaching the stated mission. Pastors and other church leaders need to be more deliberate and focused on spiritual combat training tasks. A Christian's Supreme Commander is the Lord and Savior, Jesus Christ. His "mission" is clearly stated in various places throughout Holy Scripture. Jesus said, "...Go and make disciples of all nations, baptizing them in the name of the Father and of the Son and of the Holy Spirit, teaching them to obey everything I have commanded you. And surely I am with you always, to the very end of the age." (Matthew 28: 19-20, NIV) How the disciples accomplished Christ's mission depended on their conception and execution of a "spiritual" METL.

The METL tasks for the Army are critical. Army Field Manual 25-100 states: "Battle-focused training programs are based on wartime requirements. Army organizations cannot achieve and sustain profi-ciency on every possible training task. Therefore, commanders must selectively identify the tasks that are essential to accomplishing the organization's wartime mission."[3] Part of the problem for the Church seems to be that leaders have many different understandings about the essential mission of the Church. The challenge in the Protestant Church is that there is no one leader. Protestants have no pope! While many thank God there is no papacy, Protestants often aimlessly play "hit or miss" with their essential mission because no one leader holds denominations or congregations accountable. Here, the Army's hierarchical structure is advantageous to the accomplishment of the mission. The process of developing the METL ends with the commander's imprimatur. FM 25-100 continues:

> There are two primary inputs to METL development: war plans and external directives. The most critical inputs to METL development are the organization's wartime operations and contingency plans. The missions and related information provided in these plans are key to determining essential training tasks. External directives are additional sources of training tasks that relate to an organization's wartime mission." Commanders analyze the applicable tasks contained in external directives and select for training only those tasks essential to accomplish their organization's wartime mission. This selection process reduces the number of tasks the organization must train. The compilation of tasks critical for wartime mission accomplishment is the organization's METL.[4]

Boot Camp for Believers

By definition, a METL must be clear and simple. The new book or "training manual" that is sweeping many Protestant churches is Rick Warren's *The Purpose Driven Life*. It is beautifully simple and understandable. Entire congregations in many denominations are using Warren's POI as they seek to create a Christian soldier identity or warrior ethos. Why is this book so popular? Perhaps it meets the recognized need for direction and usefulness that so many believers and congregations lack. Cynthia Woolever and Deborah Bruce's *A Field Guide to U.S. Congregations* clearly make this observation.

"Congregations, like people, live in the present. But they have a story about their past that gives meaning to today. Likewise, they have a mental map about what the future looks like. Is the future more of the same or does it look radically different?"[5]

In my experience, a large percentage of believers in American evangelical congregations never seem to go beyond their personal salvation encounter. They are stuck in purposelessness. Unaware of their recruitment as soldiers in a cosmic war against demonic terror, many Western Protestants are hopelessly enmeshed in a morass of individualism. Christians' comfort zones are hard to enlarge. Attending church is one thing, but being trained for spiritual warfare is quite another! They do not know or understand Christ's "mission" or their unique purpose in life. If believers were willing to receive their pastor's guidance in shaping a personal and congregational METL, they might be able to break out of an attitude of powerlessness and get in the war.

I assert that *The Purpose Driven Life* is, in fact, a manual that clearly compiles a Christian "mission essential task list." Warren reduces this METL to five. They are: "to love him (God), to be a part of his family, to become like him, to serve him, and to tell others about him."[6] I see the first three tasks as individual in nature. That is, the emphasis is on what one *should* do to establish basic identity in the Christian family. The next two tasks are "other" directed. *What or how* can one get into the battle line? Here is the great challenge facing U.S. congregations. What do pastors and church leaders do if their membership is simply not interested in "basic *combat* training?" Most U.S. Christians are simply not "wired" into thinking or asking what or how questions. Woolever and Bruce's surveys are instructive here, too.

What worshippers value is the best gauge of their identity. It's difficult to name one favorite, so we asked worshipers to choose up to three aspects of their congregations that they particularly value. Great diversity of opinion about the most treasured aspects of congregational life emerged. Almost half (49%) chose sharing the sacrament of Holy Communion (i.e. sharing in the Eucharist, the Lord's Supper). The second most-valued feature is the sermons, preaching, or homilies. Finally, one-third value the traditional style of worship or music characteristic of their congregation... Only 16% chose each of the following aspects as their most valued: reaching the unchurched and ministry for children and youth.[7]

Clearly, most survey respondents are very content in their desire to be spiritually fed and are not able or willing to be committed to outreach, thus fulfilling our Lord's command. If people are not interested in being trained, how are congregations going to do it? In the Army, soldiers who decline to be trained are discharged from the military as being "unsuited for military service." Sometimes commanders discover that unsuitable trainees have, in fact, been brought into service as soldiers because of a "fraudulent enlistment." Perhaps many so-called "believers" are in our churches because they were never properly enlisted. The initial presentation of the Gospel did not include the demands of discipleship. If people are not willing to be disciples in good faith, perhaps they should be "set aside" in some fashion.

Other parishioners are "planted" in congregations as infiltrators of Satan. The Apostle Paul reminds us that, "For there must also be factions among you, in order that those who are approved may have become evident among you." (1 Corinthians 11: 19, NASV) The aged apostle John also speaks about the urgency of identifying those persons in our congregations who are working against the further-ance of the Gospel and the Church's overall development. He says, "...Even now many antichrists have arisen; from this we know that is the last hour. They went out from us, but they were not really of us; for if they had been of us, they would have remained with us; but they went out, in order that it might be shown that they all are not of us" (1 John 2: 18-19, NASV). An aggressive spiritual combat oriented "boot camp" may very well flush out these impostors. In the *Book of Church Order*, the Presbyterian Church USA addresses this "confrontational" dimension of a disciple's calling. It says, "God's redeeming and reconciling activity in the world continues through the presence and power of the Holy Spirit, who confronts individuals and societies with Christ's Lordship of life and calls them to repentance and to obedience to the will of God."[8]

A "believer's boot camp" must first appeal to parishioners' sense of duty and calling. Christians must be trained in the "spiritual combatives." Believers need to know how to survive their life-long spiritual struggle. One of the greatest classics in ascetic theology is Dom Lorenzo Scupoli's book *The Spiritual Combat.* In the preface of this book, B.F. Marcetteau, the spiritual director of the Theological College of the Catholic University of America states, "The purpose of the *Spiritual Combat* is clearly stated in the First Chapter; it is to lead the soul to the summit of spiritual perfection. What is meant by spiritual perfection? We are told that it does not consist in external works and practices, but is all interior; it means knowing and loving God, despising and mastering in us all our evil inclinations, that we may be able to submit and abandon ourselves entirely to God, out of love for Him."[9] This classic book is described as "a course of spiritual strategy."[10]

In developing our prayer life, we learn that God really loves us and we can grow in our love of Him. Mel Gibson's sensational film, *The Passion of Christ*, touches this special cord about prayer in the Christian's life. The well-known magazine *Christianity Today* comments, "When Protestants talk about prayer, they usually mean talking to God about what is on their heart and asking him to deal with life's difficulties. When Catholics talk about prayer, they mean those same things, but they need to include as well certain practices of contemplation and meditation."[11] The Spiritual Warfare Movement would agree with Scupoli's emphasis on the importance of the believers' inner life, but with this twist: the value of "warfare prayer" is not at all contemplative, but rather authoritatively aggressive and confrontational. Speaking of how Jesus linked prayer with healing, Charles Kraft states, "But prayer was not his central activity when he was healing people or delivering them from demons...in his healing ministry, Jesus did not ask God for help. He simply took the authority God had given him and acted on God's behalf!"[12]

Whether contemplative or combative, a believer's training in prayer is crucial for personal growth and service for God. I believe that most Protestant Christians know very little about contemplative prayer. Scupoli is right when he emphasizes the "inner life." Unless one first possesses an inner relationship with God, how can a person pull down the "strongholds" the Apostle Paul mentions in 2 Corinthians 10:3-5? Scupoli specifies four "essential weapons" in his spiritual strategy. They are: "self-distrust; confidence in God; training in spiritual warfare through the proper use of our mental and physical powers; prayer, both short and ejaculatory, and prolonged in the form of mental prayer."[13] Whereas the "Revolution in Military Affairs" (RMA) for the army focuses on technology and more reliance on attaining complete situational awareness, the Church could benefit by fostering a "revolution in spiritual affairs" and seeking spiritual situational awareness and spiritual direction for its warriors. To do this, individual denominations and congregations must cultivate a "top to bottom" approach for attaining a more complete spiritual discernment of the times and environment around them. Believers can and should be trained to "test the spirits" (1 John 4:1).

While it is true that the Pauline Epistles speak of the importance of the spiritual gift of "distinguishing of spirits," (1 Corinthians 12:10) few believers know they may possess this "gift of the Spirit" or care about exercising it. I believe that one of the most important skills a spiritual warrior must learn is listening to God. For most people, developing reliable spiritual discernment takes a lifetime. Satan glories in his ability to deceive. As the "father of lies," he wreaks tremendous confusion and havoc. Many Christian people are rightly concerned about relying too much on a source of knowledge that can be so easily counterfeited. Because of this real danger however, Christians have neglected to even try and cultivate spiritual discernment. Healthy skepticism is one thing, but large-scale neglect of God's gifts is inexcusable.

I suppose we just have to live with some skepticism. We have been carefully taught to be skeptical especially about spiritual matters...Satan is a master counterfeiter. He cleverly imitates each of the things God does, even performing great signs and wonders 'in order to deceive even God's chosen people, if possible'. (Matthew 24:24)...The biggest challenge is to learn to listen to God. And the greatest learning happens when we hear from him and follow what we hear.[14]

The Army recruits and trains its soldiers to function in a particular job or MOS. However, the average congregation does little to assist its members to experiment, identify, and practice the "gifts of the Spirit."

Spiritual Giftedness and Finding Your Place in the Body of Christ

If there is a need for the establishment of a Christian's "Soldier's Creed" (and I believe there is), perhaps the Church should understand the importance of the "team." The Army's newly released "Soldier's Creed" states in its first sentence, "I am a warrior and a member of a team." Although the concept of "Body Life" has been known and generally accepted for years, many Christians just don't know or care that they are members of a spiritual team. They are responsible for themselves spiritually and are also accountable for ministry, not as "lone-ranger" Christians, but as members of teams.

Developing soldiers and integrating them into operational teams is the most efficient way to maximize effectiveness. To recruit soldiers with the "right stuff" requires someone who is a leader to discover persons who have certain skills or gifts. The present Army of the United States too often finds and trains soldiers for certain MOS's and then proceeds to fill a personnel slot that essentially wastes that soldier's talents and training. Soldiers in the Army get the feeling at times that they are "apprentice soldiers" instead of war-fighters. I believe that many pastors and congregations do the same thing. Too many Christians are "apprentice believers." Believers' gifts need to be discovered and then channeled into operational teams that best utilize their gifts. But before teams can be fielded, people need to be allowed to find their passion. God designs us to not only please him, but also to find pleasure in our service. I am reminded of the 1981 Oscar-winning film, *Chariots of Fire*. In that film, Eric Lidell was temporarily delayed from his God-directed mission to China in order to train and compete in the 1924 Olympics. In one scene,

Lidell explained why he loved running. Paraphrasing, he said that because God made him with the ability to run fast, he knew God took pleasure in his ability. Lidell was absolutely convinced that his passion, running, brought sheer pleasure to his Lord.

> That's not to say that winning isn't important to the competitors in Hugh Hudson's film. On the contrary, for British track stars Harold Abrahams (Ben Cross) and Eric Lidell (Ian Charleson), it's a paramount concern, but neither is so obsessed by their goal that they lose sight of the larger picture. Eric is a devout Christian who runs because he believes it glorifies God. Harold is a Jew who competes as a way of proving his worth. Both are driven by an inner fire, and have nothing but respect for their rivals.[15]

Finding that "inner fire" or passion is precisely the first step in discovering one's spiritual gift. Far too many Christians settle for a humdrum existence because they either are afraid to discover and use their spiritual gifts or have never been in circumstances where they were "discovered, developed and deployed."[16] Despite the fact that the Army often just fills slots with bodies, drill sergeants and other members of the cadre are responsible for producing soldiers who are motivated, disciplined, and competent. At least in BCT and AIT training, the coaching atmosphere is called the "Insist/Assist" philosophy. The Army's sergeants have tremendous motivational power. The Church also needs many more leaders who "insist" that members under their charge discover their spiritual giftedness and then "assist" them to become productive members of operational teams. It is the Church that is obligated by its Lord to "equip" its members rather than just assign them responsibilities they are not suited or gifted to accomplish. Wayne Cordeiro says, "Assigning someone to a task and equipping that person for the same are completely different issues."[17]

Christian churches need to get over their fear of thinking outside the box. Most local congregations are fear-bound and paralyzed in realizing their potential. The Army, like most huge institutions, is not known for creative innovation and responsiveness to change.

Perhaps that is why a unique organization like the U.S. Defense Advanced Research Projects Agency (DARPA) exists. The hallmark of DARPA is its mandate to "spur radical innovation that translates into overwhelming battlefield domination."[18] This agency has as its incredible goal "to make a third of the country's military forces completely autonomous and unmanned by 2015."[19] Can the Church discover, develop, and deploy teams of people to accomplish similarly monumental projects? I believe it can *if* it is willing to move beyond traditionalism and begin equipping and mobilizing spiritual warrior teams.

...What is of more interest to us in doing church as a team is the use of the word 'equipping.' The role of these offices is not to corner the market on ministry but, rather, to equip *God's people* to do the work of the ministry.

The Greek word translated as 'equipping' in Ephesians 4:12 is very picturesque. It is the word *katartismos*, from the verb meaning 'to mend.' The word is earlier found in Mark 1: 19, which shows the brothers James and John in a boat with their father, Zebedee, mending their nets. James and John were mending their nets, equipping themselves to catch more fish.[20]

The best example of this concept in action is a church I discovered in Colorado Springs, Colorado, called New Life Church. I became acquainted with this dynamic congregation while participating in C. Peter Wagner's Doctor of Ministry class, entitled "New Apostolic Paradigms." After reading all the prerequisite literature for this course, I received the most benefit from Pastor Ted Haggard's lecture on July 17, 1998. Haggard clearly set forth a number of philosophical and theological presuppositions that outlined his vision for ministry. There can be no doubt that Haggard is an extremely gifted spiritual leader. His heart's desire is to reach his city and the world for Jesus Christ! In his book *Church for the Unchurched*, George G. Hunter III describes another church that expresses the vision and atmosphere at New Life Church as well:

Another growing church stresses that the people are the ministers and the pastors are the administrators. The pastor explains it this way, 'The staff make most of the necessary administrative decisions, thus freeing the laity from the consuming involvements that immobilize, divide, and exhaust most congregations, thereby freeing the people's time and energy for ministry and outreach in the community.' The goal for that church is to turn an audience into an army. ...Jesus did not tell the world to go to church. He told the church to go to the world.[21]

The Church needs to use its soldiers more effectively. Unlocking the people's passions and energies is the key to accomplishing its mission. Cordeiro continues with his understanding of what must be done on a large scale.

Under the traditional template of how church is done, the pastor does the work of ministry and he gets as many people as he can to help him. In doing church as a team, the people do the work of ministry—and they get the pastor to help them! That not only sounds better—it's biblical![22]

Even though the Army talks about the "team" and the necessity of being team players, the process of developing teams through a deliberate mentorship program is woefully lacking. Junior leaders who crave a more personal relationship with their superiors are often very disappointed. It is one of the reasons why junior leaders are leaving the Army. The Army is very reluctant to use the term because it connotes a classical "relational" concept. The term "mentor" is actually derived from the character named Mentor, who was a faithful friend of the Greek hero Odysseus in Homer's epic story, *The Odyssey*. When Odysseus went off to war, he left Mentor behind to serve as tutor to his son, Telemachus. Mentor served in this role, earning a reputation as being wise, sober, and loyal.[23] Because of the close personal relationship that is required for classical mentoring to take place, the senior leadership in the Army is reluctant to implement a formal mentorship program.

In the classic sense, mentorship implies more than just good leadership. It involves a more senior or experienced person taking a substantial personal (in addition to professional) interest in a junior, less-experienced person's future. The mentor is a guide, a sage, with important advice and experience that he or she voluntarily bestows upon the protégé. This personal aspect is important, as the classic notion of mentorship implies a genuine fondness and respect between the mentor and the protégé... When this mutual attraction, respect, and interest exist, then a voluntary mentoring relationship can develop in the classic understanding of the term.[24]

Many commanders are adamantly opposed to a mentorship scheme that even hints at favoritism. The cultivation of relationships between senior level leaders and subordinates outside of operational matters is anathema.

In the Church of Jesus Christ, close personal relationships are critically necessary in order for the world to be attracted to the Gospel message. The Scripture says, "By this all men will know that you are my disciples, if you love for one another" (John 13:35, NIV). If the Church is to transition into this "new church paradigm," a complete transformation must take place in how the senior pastors model and mentor less experienced ministers and laypeople. In an article entitled "Is Spiritual Mentoring a Biblical Idea," the author Lynn Anderson states the following:

Admittedly, the word does not appear in the Bible... Cultural anthropologists tell us that almost every society has had 'elders' of some kind. Whether they be tribal chieftains, village head-men, clan leaders or family patriarchs—most every social unit across history and around the globe has clearly recognized adult role-models or Wisdom Figures... However, until recently this role is conspicuously absent from modern American culture, at least in formal social structures...We long for mentors.[25]

Monitoring and Mentoring

In civilian ministry, I have had only one experience in an "associate" pastoral position. It was a disaster! Hoping to be mentored at this early juncture in my ministry, I discovered after six months that the senior pastor was adamantly opposed to an associate pastor even being hired by the congregation. Needless to say, very little positive mentoring took place. My pastoral association with the congregation was dissolved after only ten months! The thoroughly negative experience has left emotional scars to this day. Even though the Church expresses the desire for close, personal mentoring relationships, bitter rivalries and sinful behavior often is the norm. Jesus also had to frequently referee between jealous and intensely competitive disciples. The key is in acquiring and sustaining the right attitude between pastoral and lay colleagues. Anderson comments, "This, of course, means that spiritual leaders are to be identified in a radically different way and upon different criterion than leaders are usually recognized in other arenas: business, military, politics, athletics. Spiritual leaders are not necessarily to be admired on the basis of their business administration skills or their entrepreneurial leadership, but because of their shepherd hearts! They have a servant life-style."[26]

In many organizations, the leadership climate, or what the Army calls, "command climate," is very demoralized and relationally poisoned. The Army and the Church state similar doctrinal beliefs in fostering and preserving climates of collegiality and respect. In actual practice, both institutions suffer from confused and chaotic leader-subordinate relationships. The Army War College article plaintively asserts, "Although doctrine and stated beliefs indicate that these components of leadership are desirable and good, surveys indicate that the Army's collective behavior is falling short of expectations. Army leaders at all levels should renew efforts to reduce the gap between stated beliefs and actual practice."[27] Perhaps the real problem is not in the "leadership" at all but in an inadequate understanding and practice of "followership."

Paul the apostle also, spelled out mentoring as his leadership model very simply. 'Follow my example as I follow the example of Christ.' (1 Corinthians 11:1) 'Whatever you have learned or received or heard from me, or seen in me—put into practice.' (Philippians 4:9) In other words, let me mentor you. Let me be your role model...Example! Teach! Model! These are all facets of mentoring which is an indispensable tool in developing fully devoted followers of Jesus and in transmitting the faith from one generation to the next.[28]

In order to develop "fully devoted followers of Jesus," the Church needs non-commissioned officers (NCOs) or sergeants. These soldiers are literally the "linchpin" of all the Army is and does. These individuals are specifically chosen and trained to provide connections between the common foot soldier and the officers who command. Especially in combat arms units in the Army, (infantry, armor, artillery) these NCOs are what the Bible refers to as "mighty men."

The great Old Testament saint, David, demonstrated his followership long before his leadership. He obediently cared for the family's sheep, played his music at the king's command, and was known as a loyal soldier in King Saul's army. When David became a famous general, he acknowledged that the reason he won battles was because of soldiers whom he called the 'Mighty Men' who had developed followership to an art.[29]

The Need for Sergeants in the Church

These "Mighty Men" mentioned in 1 Samuel 23:8f were a special group of thirty professional soldiers who lived a creed that prided themselves on their soldier skills and their care of the ordinary soldiers under their charge. In today's Army, NCOs learn and quickly internalize the "NCO Creed" upon attaining the rank of Sergeant. In part, the creed says, "Officers of my unit will have maximum time to accomplish their duties; they will not have to accomplish mine. I will earn their respect and confidence as well as that of my soldiers... I will exercise initiative by taking appropriate action in the absence of orders..."[30] These Sergeants fulfill a training and communication function with relatively new soldiers who need a great deal of supervision. The Army views these mid-level soldiers in much more than a management capacity. While serving as the standard bearers of discipline, they also empower and facilitate younger and less experienced soldiers in the accomplishment of their mission. NCOs constantly seek ways to increase the professional development of their trainees. Their penchant for education means the realization of their soldiers' true potential. In the Non-Commissioned Officer's Guide are these words: "Education is the *constant* (Italics mine) watchword of the NCO. It is the duty of the NCO to learn the job at the next highest rank in case he must eventually fulfill that role. A good NCO realizes that there is always more to learn."[31] "King David's 'Mighty Men' were not just war heroes but can be credited with participating in "the divinely ordained salvation. These soldier-leaders were highly valued because they fought against Saul's evil schemes and stood with David in a 'Holy War.'"[32] I believe these exemplary "holy warriors" functioned as senior non-commissioned officers, namely sergeants, who prided themselves on fulfilling the mission regardless of the hardships.

Why would sergeants benefit the Church? God honors the efforts of "mighty men." These men are so single-minded that nothing will stop them from spiritual victory! Acting as liaisons between the formalized leadership of a congregation and the "ordinary" membership, spiritual sergeants would be able to provide first-line oversight and shepherding of believers from the early stages of their regeneration through beginning discipleship stages. As NCOs in the Army "insist and assist" on certain behaviors and actions of their trainees, so spiritual sergeants must be identified, nurtured, and then enabled to equip and energize parishioners for spiritual fights. In my thirty-two years of pastoral experience, I have found that most local congregations have very few "mighty men." In many Presbyterian congregations and U.S. Army Chapel programs, it is the women's groups that far surpass the men's groups in providing any spiritual leadership. Organizations like *Promise Keepers* are seeking to reverse this trend by challenging men to be spiritual warriors. Indeed, many parachurch groups are aggressively seeking to sustain the spiritually wounded and restore them to the battlefield. Many men and women in our churches are suffering from great spiritual pain. Both men and women are needed to be spiritual sergeants so that the individual and collective woundedness of believers is addressed. It is fundamentally a "shepherding" function that demands spiritual wisdom and thoroughness.

All spiritual leaders are to be "shepherding" their people after the example of Jesus. Speaking after the miraculous feeding of the five thousand, the Gospel of *Mark* records, "When Jesus landed and saw a large crowd, he had compassion on them, because they were like sheep without a shepherd. So he began teaching them many things" (Mark 6:34, NIV). Jesus knew there was a relationship between healing physical, emotional, and spiritual wounds and sound Biblical instruction. An electronic devotional provided by Neil Eskelin brings the shepherd-sheep metaphor into focus.

While driving through Israel I came across a scene that could have been painted thousands of years earlier. We pulled to the side of the road to watch a solitary shepherd who was faithfully keeping watch over his flock of several hundred sheep. He was crouched down, holding a staff in his hand, rarely allowing his eyes to wander. The sheep, foraging for nourishment, didn't seem to notice their master. You can rest assured, however, they knew his exact location and the reason for his presence. As a parent, teacher or executive, you have also been given an assignment that carries a heavy responsibility. And while it is true that many decisions are allowed to be made at lower levels on the chain of command, people continue to look to the top for both direction and protection.

True leaders come to the realization that their sheep were not created to be sheared, or to be served as lamb chops or mutton stew. They are unique individuals who have great expectations about their shepherd. It is a defining moment when someone in authority finally reaches the conclusion that leadership is not about using people. It's about serving them.[33]

The sustaining presence of the shepherd provides another reality concerning spiritual warfare. Often, people are hurt along their spiritual journey. How does God want people to treat the wounded among us? Perhaps insights can be gained from the Army Medical Department's care of soldiers on and off the battlefield?

PART V. SUSTAINING THE FORCE
CHAPTER EIGHT

THE PRACTICE OF BATTLEFIELD MEDICINE AND THE ARMY MEDICAL DEPARTMENT

The preeminent object of any battlefield medical treatment procedure is to return the soldier to duty as soon as possible. Combatants are needed in the line. In the United States Army, Field Manual 8-10-6, which deals with *Principles of Health Service Support Operations*, outlines numerous basic rules of care. They are: conformity, continuity, control, proximity, flexibility, mobility, and prevention.[1]

The Army Health Services' motto found on its official crest summarizes what is most important. It reads: *To Conserve the Fighting Strength*. The "conservation" effort then is intended to treat soldiers who are wounded, sick, or emotionally disabled in order to restore and sustain the fighting force. There can be no greater priority in war or peace than to provide both preventive and efficient reactive medical care to America's soldiers.

It was my privilege to be assigned to two different Army medical centers during my chaplain career. While professionally observing the care of the Army Medical Department (AMEDD) and receiving significant emergency surgical care myself, I learned to respect the technical skills and compassion of the Army medical staff. In a previous Doctor of Ministry course entitled MG714 "Deep Healing and Deliverance," I briefly addressed some of the principles that AMEDD employs:

> The principle of "Continuity" first peaks my interest because it addresses the absolute necessity of providing quality health care to soldiers regardless of where they may be in the world. As defined in the section, *Principles of Health Service Support Operations* in Army Field Manual 8-10-6, continuity is 'Health service support that is continuous since an interruption of treatment may cause an increase in morbidity and mortality. Procedures are standardized at each level to ensure that all required medical treatment at that level be accomplished. No patient is evacuated any farther to the rear than his physical condition or the military situation requires.'[2]

The primary goal then of the AMEDD in treating its battlefield wounded is to transport and medically intervene in the life of a patient so that the soldier can be returned as soon as possible to active duty. The process is designed to quickly identify and classify injury or illness and to apply the necessary treatment procedures. The U.S. Army Field Manual 8-35, *Evacuation of the Sick and Wounded* states, "Medical evacuation is the process of transporting while providing essential medical care any sick, injured, or wounded person to or between medical treatment facilities. The medical evacuation and treatment of the sick and wounded *begin at the place of injury or onset of illness* (Italics mine) and continue as far rearward as the medical condition of the patient requires. The military medical services accomplish these functions as rapidly and effectively as possible keeping the welfare of the patient as the primary concern.[3]

The Importance of Triage

In the midst of a battle, the rapid identification, classification, transport, and treatment of wounded is an exceedingly complex undertaking. In order to expedite the process, a tried and true *triage* process has been established to classify injury or illness. One definition of triage is "a process for sorting injured people into groups based on their need for or likely benefit from immediate medical treatment."[4]

Medical triage developed from the need to prioritize the care of injured soldiers in battlefield settings. The concept of prioritizing patients and providing immediate care to the most seriously injured was practiced in France in the early 1800s (triage is derived from the French *trier*, meaning "to sort"). Over the next century, this practice was further developed in armies throughout the world. As a result, many injured persons whose surgery theretofore might have been delayed received critical care earlier. During World War I, improved outcomes of some battle injuries were credited to appropriate triage. Thus, triage is one of the first applications of medical care after first aid.[5]

We accept the need for deliberate, decisive, and impartial triage actions on military battlefields. We instinctively trust doctors, nurses, and medics who efficiently separate wounded into treatment categories. Life and death decisions are made using triage. The AMEDD's technological processes are in place to transform the identification and treatment of its wounded.

Critical to the overall Army Transformation Program is the acquisition of informational dominance that allows commanders complete situational awareness on the battlefield. When dealing with battlefield injuries, a commander needs to quickly and accurately know the medical status of his or her ground troops. One of the Army's principal initiatives is called "Force XXI." This effort seeks to "digitize" all the soldier and equipment assets at a commander's disposal for future conflicts of the twenty-first century. One of the most exciting and life-saving efforts is the increasingly computer-ized and near instantaneous flow of medical information now made available to Army medical personnel as the battlefield injury actually occurs.

Digitization of the new Force XXI Division is a high priority. Digitization is defined as the application of information to acquire, exchange, and employ timely battlefield information. It will *enhance situational understanding* and provide the means for information dominance by enabling friendly forces... to *share a common picture of the battlefield* while communicating and targeting in real or near realtime.

Digitization will reduce the fog of war and *decrease decision-making time* by *optimizing the flow of information.* It will allow the orchestration of combat power at critical times and places faster than an adversary can...[6]

The AMEDD of the twenty-first century seeks to "optimize" the flow of medical information in order to allow commanders to reduce critical decision-making time during the heat of battle. The emphasis on "seamless communications" intends to establish a medical information system so sophisticated and speedy that when soldiers become ill or injured, all of their vital signs are immediately transmitted to the appropriate medic or battlefield aid station. Because the evacuation system begins "at the place of injury," doctors can gain valuable time as they seek to stabilize and intervene with suitable treatment. Future soldiers may actually be physically "enhanced" in order to sustain individual combat efficiency.

The military feels a moral imperative to do whatever is necessary to make sure that each soldier comes home alive and well. If it takes genetic, cybernetic, or nanotechnological modifications to do that, so be it. After all, how could we deny our soldiers the greatest chance of survival? ...It's only a matter of time before members of the armed forces will be required to undergo other forms of augmentation.[7]

These incredible life-saving technologies are no substitute for "hands on" intervention. One of the best means the army employs is through the "Combat Life-Saver" (CLS) program.

Combat Life Savers

In 1988, I received CLS training at Fort Drum, New York. Advanced first aid skills equipped me to provide a paraprofessional presence and quick reaction force for critical situations. The realistic training provided a useful object lesson on the importance of caring for one's fellow soldier. The watchword is "buddy care." Soldiers know that the CLS training could save their life also!

Getting first aid to wounded soldiers has always been dangerous, since it is danger that got the soldier hurt in the first place. The '91B' or Combat Medic attached to every infantry platoon is a very over-worked person who may be targeted by an unethical enemy wearing the proper red-cross armband. The U.S. Army's Combat Life-Saver (CLS) Program is an excellent initiative to get a soldier in every squad-sized unit skilled and equipped to perform emergency life saving medical tasks; like starting inter-venous lines... These lines are vital for prompt replacement of fluids lost to injuries.

CLSers are to bridge the gap from self-aid or buddy aid (SABA) training every soldier receives and the platoon Aidman (91B Combat medic). The fluid, non-linear battle-field requires that injured soldiers get treated immediately and their condition stabilized, not wait for another level of care to treat them which is often too late.[8]

Combat lifesavers are considered by the Army to be "first responders" when dealing with battle or non-battle injuries (NBI). The Army's experience dictates that "Global casualty care manage-ment and evacuation provides continuous essential care, to treat casualties and return them to duty, or stabilize them in theater and evacuate to the appropriate level of care. Treatment begins with the 'First Responder' (self-aid/buddy-aid, combat lifesaver advanced first aid, combat medic care), supporting basic prevention and caring, for both disease and non-battle injury (DNBI) and combat casualties, as quickly and as close to the point of injury as possible."[9] Army medical personnel pride themselves on being committed and able to "rapidly detect, assess, and diagnose disease and illness...maintaining effective, continuous operations under all battlefield conditions."[10] Doctors, nurses, medics, combat lifesavers, and others are positioned according to Army doctrine as far forward as possible in order to decrease the treatment time for wounded soldiers. When soldiers know that people are close by to provide physical and emotional care, they perform their soldierly duties better and morale improves.

Collecting and Treating Casualties

The AMEDD's "standard of care" is "to effectively provide individual relief, while clearing the battlefield of all casualties, thus permitting the warfighter to continue the battle unencumbered. Responsive far-forward resuscitation, stabilization, and timely/rapid evacuation, particularly casualties with major trauma, not only affect the availability of the fighting force, but also impact the morale and readiness of the unit at large."[11] The perpetual challenge of course of any casualty collection operation is to "recognize, assess and stabilize"[12] the patient. Speed is paramount. The United States Army uses a robust array of people and materiel to conduct evacuation operations. Army Field Manual 1-113 states:

> Commanders of medical units in a theater of operations use their resources to effectively evacuate and treat sick, injured, and wounded soldiers. Whether a soldier survives when wounded on the battlefield often depends on the time it takes to receive treatment. Quick responsive care is essential to protecting the force.[13]

It is extremely important for the reader to note the concepts of being far forward, quick-responsiveness, rapid assessment, and stabilization. Battlefield wounded should expect that caregivers will do everything necessary and within their power to treat them. The Army's medical evacuation system places the primary responsibility for casualty evacuation on the soldier's unit. For soldiers, that is the company. According to FM 1-113, "Company level care is primarily vested in the unit 1SG and XO. The 1SG ensures that combat life-savers have the required equipment on hand, and that company transportation, if available, is prepared to move casualties."[14] The AMEDD's system is deliberately designed as a "tiered" system that enables patient care to proceed upwardly to more intensive treatment. There are four levels of care. They are: (1) Care organic to the unit designed to stabilize the patient, (2) Care rendered at a medical clearing station, (3) Care rendered at a Medical Treatment Facility (MTF), and (4) Care rendered at a hospital or medical center equipped for general and specialized procedures.[15]

Perhaps the teaching point is that soldiers wounded or ill are rapidly identified "at the point of injury" and progressively evacuated to appropriate treatment personnel and facilities. The Army does all in its power to respect its injured soldiers, especially its combat wounded. It will move "heaven and earth" to leave no wounded, dead, or imprisoned soldier behind.

Soldiers taken prisoner require special care and are deserving of special honor. Almost five years, ago I had the distinct privilege of meeting Senator John McCain as he was campaigning for the Presidency in South Carolina. After telling him briefly of my father's POW experience, he said, "You must be proud of him." I told him that I was indeed proud. McCain's best-selling book, *Faith of My Fathers*, speaks about the importance of faith and loyalty. His reflection on his own five and a half years as a prisoner in North Vietnam speaks volumes about maintaining one's faith in God and his faith in the values of his country.

Our senior officers always stressed to us the three essential keys to resistance, which we were to keep uppermost in our mind, especially in moments when we were isolated or otherwise deprived of their guidance and the counsel of other prisoners. They were faith in God, faith in country, and faith in your fellow prisoners. The purpose of our captors' inhumanity to us was nothing less than to force our descent into a world of total faithlessness; a world with no God, no country, no loyalty. Our faith would be replaced with simple reliance on the sufferance of our antagonists. Without faith, we would lose our dignity, and live among our enemies as animals lived among their human masters... Hungry, beaten, hurt, scared, and alone, human beings can begin to feel that they are removed from God's love, a vast distance separating them from their Creator.[16]

The Tradition of Leaving No Wounded Behind

The concept of "leaving no one behind" applies primarily to the notion of abandoning a "fallen" comrade on the field of battle. It is a direct reference to the famed *Ranger Creed*. The creed's relevant portion reads:

Never shall I fail my comrades. I will always keep myself mentally alert, physically strong and morally straight and I will shoulder more than my share of the task whatever it may be...

Energetically will I meet the enemies of my Country. I shall defeat them on the field of battle for I am better trained and will fight with all my might. Surrender is not a Ranger word. *I will never leave a fallen comrade to fall into the hands of the enemy* (Italics mine) and under no circumstances will I ever embarrass my country.[17]

Although the Rangers are elite soldiers, this creed has through military tradition, been incorporated throughout the armed services as being an ideal worthy of America's fighting forces. In order to actualize this tradition, the military services sometimes have to justify some uncomfortable facts.

On Wed., Mar. 6, Operation Anaconda hit a snag. A United States Navy Seal fell out of his helicopter over the Afghan mountains and was quickly dragged away by enemy forces. Risking their lives to save the body of their comrade, soldiers pursued the enemy fighters, eventually retrieving the body after a 12-hour chase. The victory, however, did not come without losses. By day's end, six American soldiers had been killed and 12 had been wounded.[18]

Colonel Ellis Golson, former Executive Officer in charge of the quick reaction 1993 force that retrieved killed and wounded soldiers in Mogadishu, Somalia, had some pointed observations to make. The *Yale Herald* raised the cost-benefit ratio of putting living soldiers at risk to rescue injured comrades or even to recover dead bodies from behind enemy lines.[19] Colonel Golson responded, "It never crossed any-body's mind [to debate the policy]. You're an eternal optimist. Even if there's one guy you can take back, then it's worth it to take back one… It's a code of ethics, a way of life. It's part of the culture of being in the military, that you are a cohesive unit. And you don't leave anyone behind."[20] I believe Colonel Golson is correct. This "no one left behind policy" is a code that all servicemen and women know and accept. The value that Americans place on one human life frequently collides with politics and other competing considerations.

I believe there is a moral and ethical chasm existing in this country. The Founding Fathers' values for America are under attack. Many theologians and philosophers have raised the alarm for the past twenty-five years. Perhaps the most striking commentary on America's ideal versus real value system came in 1978 from Russian writer Aleksandr Solzhenitsyn. In a *Christianity Today* article, Solzhenitsyn is quoted from his Harvard University Commencement address entitled "A World Split Apart."

In the last three centuries, all moral and spiritual limitations, all notions of duty and sacrifice, have slowly been discarded in the West. While we've safeguarded human rights, man's sense of responsibility to God and society grew dimmer and dimmer...We have lost the concept of a Supreme Complete Entity which used to restrain our passions and our irresponsibility. We have placed too much hope in political and social reforms, only to find out that we were being deprived of our most precious possession: our spiritual life.[21]

The editors of *Christianity Today* further comment on America's "not (so) godly system."

This is not a godly system, though it is a system under God-or more precisely, under God's judgment. The prophetic words spoken against Israel long ago are tragically timely: "Ah, sinful nation, people laden with iniquity, offspring who do evil, children who deal corruptly, who have forsaken the Lord...The whole head is sick, and the whole heart faint. From the sole of the foot even to the head, there is no soundness in it, but bruises and sores and bleeding wounds" (Isaiah 1: 4-6). [22]

CHAPTER NINE

THE CHURCH AND ITS WOUNDED

It is not a revolutionary idea that the Church of Jesus Christ is under attack or frequently suffering from various "wounds." From the very beginning, Satan has attempted to deceive, divide, injure, and eventually destroy people who desire to know and follow God. It is my contention, however, that many followers of Christ are dangerously unaware of three things. First, many simply either don't know or refuse to believe that professing faith in Christ places them squarely on the front lines of a cosmic war. Second, many Christians are ill equipped to fight such a war. They do not have significant knowledge of their spiritual weapons arsenal. Third, many Christians are tremendously wounded and suffering great "spiritual pain" and are thus unable to engage the enemy. They are what the U.S. Army calls "combat ineffective." If the Gospel is to penetrate the hearts of billions of people, the Church must accurately portray a message that is consistent with Holy Scripture. The Bible is not reticent about demonstrations of supernatural power. The message of the cross is one that reminds us that God "is the same yesterday, today and forever." (Hebrews 13:8) The New Testament is not shy about recounting how the early Church grew. It grew because its message was relevant. People everywhere are physically, emotionally, and spiritually wounded. Human beings need healing and deliverance. Satan knows that when Christians take the message of the

New Testament seriously, his time is short. The adversary is waging an all-out offensive against the people of God. Battle casualties may mount before the return of Christ. Satan is endeavoring to nullify or create an impotent church.[1] Satan is a mass producer of spiritual "weapons of mass destruction," (WMD) bent on an all-out preemptive attack on God's people.

Understanding Spiritual Injury and Pain

Medical personnel in the U.S. Army strive to "conserve the fighting strength" of the force. Should Christian "healers" do any less in their efforts to preserve and restore emotional, spiritual, and physical health? I believe that what the Church really needs are spiritual "combat-medics/flight surgeons." Some years ago, I had occasion to meet Colonel (Doctor) Rhonda Cornum, who is a decorated Persian Gulf War veteran. She is also a former prisoner of war, having been shot down by the Iraqi Army. In her book, *She Went to War,* Doctor Cornum recounts her duties as a flight surgeon flying over enemy territory. She was taken prisoner while several of her fellow soldiers were killed. In her book, Cornum sets the record straight about the real purpose of flight surgeons or combat medics.

As stated in the motto, the goal of military medicine is to 'conserve the fighting strength' of the armed forces. Over the years, I have seen the positive impact 'medics' can have on morale and readiness, but it was dramatic during the deployment to the Middle East. Major Jonathan Letterman, a surgeon in the Union Army, said it best more than a hundred years ago. Letterman said, "A corps of medical officers was not established solely for the purpose of attending the wounded and sick. ...The labors of medical officers cover a more extended field. The leading idea, which should constantly be kept in view, is to strengthen the hand of the Commanding General.[2]

The "Spiritual Warfare Movement" (SWM) espouses a kind of spiritual flight surgeon mission for the Church. SWM adherents like

154

Charles Kraft, C. Peter Wagner, and others firmly believe that the only way to unlock billions of Muslims, Hindus, Buddhists, and others in the 10/70 window to the Gospel is to aggressively train, equip, and deploy a new breed of spiritual warrior. These warriors for Christ will assault satanic fortifications and liberate countless millions entrenched in spiritual bondage. As a result, our "Commander's" hand is strengthened. Spiritual rapid deployment forces, always on standby, are frequently dispatched to the frontlines. Advocates of the SWM are endeavoring to employ spiritual weapons and an intensely pastoral deliverance ministry in order to treat spiritual injury and pain. By barraging satanic strongholds with prayer and other spiritually assertive tactics, proponents of the SWM will weaken Satan's defensive fortifications. It should be remembered, however, that it is Jesus alone who "*destroys* the devil's work" (1 John 3:8, NIV). Only Christ can employ weapons to annihilate "Apollyon." It seems that we believers can indeed thwart satanic activity, but are not permitted to destroy the Destroyer. The all-inclusive pain and injury Satan instigates profoundly affects the bodies, minds, and spirits of human beings. For the sake of this book, I wish to focus on spiritual pain/injury and then discuss spiritual triage and intervention methods.

What do spiritual pain and injury mean? Rod Burton, writing in *The Journal of Pastoral Care*, says that spiritual pain from the Hospice Movement's perspective, "arises when [the patient's] view of [their] spiritual life and [their] experience of life are in a state of mismatch or conflict."[3] Burton, quoting Milton W. Hay in his article "Building Spiritual Assessment Tools," describes the nature of spiritual pain:

> Hay, writing from within a similar environment, and almost concurrently with the author of that (Hospice) Training Manual characterized spiritual suffering or pain as including: constant and chronic pain; withdrawal or isolation from spiritual support systems; conflict with family members, friends, or support staff; anxiety, fear, or mistrust of family, physicians, and hospice staff; anger, depression; self-loathing; hopelessness; feelings of failure in respect of

one" life; lack of sense of humor; unforgiveness; despair; and fear/dread.[4]

While spiritual pain is quite noticeable, it is less easily defined. Burton further explores what is called, "The Dark Night of the Sense and the Spirit."

Noticing the difference between a sense of 'consolation' and one of 'desolation' might mark the beginnings of an ability to recognize the state of one's spirit; the extent of its discomfort, even pain, or its well being. The 'Dark Night of the Sense' — that experience of dryness, of anxiety about one's relationship with God, and of the inability or disinclination to practice discursive meditation, associated with the death of one's 'false self'...

When all "felt" mystical experiences of God subside and disappear, one's relationship with God is no longer nourished through the external senses or through reason, there is an habitual sense of God's absence, (i.e. Dark Night of the Spirit) even if not guilty, of every evil.[5]

While spiritual pain exhibits itself through alienation and a hopeless state of disinterest in God, "spiritual injury" takes a devastating toll. What are these injuries?

A 'Spiritual Injury' is our response to an event caused by self, or an event beyond our control, that damages our relationship with God, self and other, and alienates us from that which gives meaning to our lives. The word injury is intentionally used. Other words such as spiritual distress, wound or hurt could have been chosen. As in an accident where bodily injury is sustained, the injury can be self-inflicted or caused by self intentionally or carelessly, or the injury can be caused by no fault of our own. Such events beyond our control are often fatalistically labeled acts of God...and just as physical injury tears at or destroys bodily tissue, so spiritual injury destroys or weakens spiritual tissue. Our connectedness to God, other or self is weakened, damaged or destroyed. The word injury carries with it a moral or ethical dimension, as in injury to one's reputation. It is a word that is also used interpersonally, as in an injury to his pride. The concept of spiritual injury therefore connotes a personal, interpersonal, moral and sacred dimension missing in bio-psycho-social explanations of human behavior...

The eight spiritual injuries are (1) guilt, (2) anger or resentment, (3) grief or sadness, (4) lack of meaning or purpose, (5) despair or hopelessness, (6) feeling that God/life has been unfair, (7) religious doubt or disbelief, and (8) fear of death.[6]

It is my contention that, just as a combat medic or CLS rapidly attends to physical injuries in combat at their point of injury, so the Church needs to train and commission "spiritual flight surgeons." Wounded and injured Christians or others in the sphere of concern of a local congregation must be more intentionally identified and "treated." In recent years, clinically trained hospital chaplains have implemented various spiritual assessment tools during certified clinical pastoral education programs. While assigned as a chaplain clinician at Eisenhower Army Medical Center in Fort Gordon, Georgia, I had occasion to briefly use a spiritual assessment tool. Hospital patients were carefully assessed regarding the presence or lack thereof of spiritual injury or issue. While hospital chaplains conducted their ministries from instinct or intuition in the past, a new era has dawned in this day of "managed care."

The importance of assessing religious beliefs or personal problems from a pastoral perspective was given renewed attention by Paul Pruyser in his book, *The Minister as Diagnostician.*[7] Not only did Pruyser emphasize the unique perspective ministers and chaplains bring to understanding human personality and problems, but he also contended that many problems were spiritual and required intervention and treatment that was religious in nature. But before treatment could begin, it was necessary that an accurate religious diagnosis be made in order for therapy to be given that was appropriate and responded to the unique problem brought to the pastor's or chaplain's attention.

While Paul Pruyser brought the critical and discerning eye of the clinician into pastoral care, Lawrence Seidl of the Catholic Health Association of the United States has introduced pastoral care to the language and process of quality assurance.[8] Seidl argues that 'all departments within the hospital, in the very near future, will be required to show that their services provide a measurable, significant outcome.' This includes pastoral care. The means by which this will be accomplished include the collection of quantitative data the assessment of spiritual needs, and planned interventions or treatments targeted to meet these needs.

While Lawrence Seidl challenges pastoral caregivers to use the tools of quality assurance to document the value of spiritual care, Larry VandeCreek invites us to use the instruments of empirical science and research to provide measurable, significant outcomes resulting from the provision of quality pastoral care.[9]

One such online assessment tool is called the "Manual for Living Water's Computer Assessment Program."

This pastoral care computer assessment program manual was developed for use with the spiritual assessment program developed by Living Water Software Corporation. It is to be used to understand, run, interpret, and use Living Water's Computer Assessment Program (LW CAP) to diagnose, treat and research mental and physical illness from the perspective of spiritual values, beliefs and practices. Its intention is to better understand the role of religious faith in the maintenance of health, the healing of diseases, and the coping with chronic illness and losses in peoples' lives.[10]

Hospitals seek to provide "measurable" outcomes from the treatment they provide. All staff sections are increasingly held accountable and certified by what is called the Joint Commission on Accreditation of Hospital Organizations (JCAHO). I received specific training in the use of a spiritual evaluative tool from the Army's MEDCOM entitled, "Multi-level Spiritual Assessment Training." (MLSA)[11] This spiritual assessment screening tool revolutionized how pastoral care was conceptualized, provided, and documented. A chaplain or other pastoral caregiver asks patients thirteen assessment questions. Some of these questions are: How would you rate your spiritual health? How would you classify your spiritual life? How much is your spiritual life a source of strength and comfort? Have the following spiritual losses or spiritual life changes occurred for you in the past year?[12] The specific information gleaned from the patient included: their religious preference and activity, perception of religious "loss/change," two sources of religious help, and three highest values. Each of these spiritual assessment categories are "scored" and tabulated. Scores are delineated for: (1) Organizational Religious Activity, (2) Non-organizational activity, and (3) a Total Religious Index.

The desired goal in treating spiritually injured people is predicated on establishing trust between the patient and the pastoral caregiver. It is my contention that the Church desperately needs spiritual combat medics or flight surgeons to aggressively and proactively triage spiritual injuries in such a way as to enhance the overall self-worth of individuals and then to petition Jesus to heal them. The Army Medical Department treats people "at the point of injury." Christ does the same. He is more willing to heal than we know. The same proactive care should be provided to Christian "soldiers" that the U.S. Army gives to its troops. I believe that denominational church executives and other spiritually gifted and trained parishioners need to be challenged to identify and treat many more spiritually and emotionally traumatized people. In the Church and society there are a very great number of people who suffer in silence for years! Many, including pastors, labor with very heavy guilt and poor self-worth issues. Satan likes things this way. Satan desires to permanently break down a person's will and self-esteem.

Dr. Neil Anderson in his book *Victory Over Darkness* says, "Satan will try to convince you that you are an unworthy, unacceptable, sin-sick person who will never amount to anything in God's eyes."[13] The Bible labels Satan as expressing "lying wonders." (2 Thessalonians 2:9) I believe that there are at least four distinct areas where Satan spreads his poisonous lies. These objectives represent his principle strategic objectives. They are: (1) To inflict "father wounds"; (2) To foster spiritual "battle fatigue"; (3) To contaminate people with unforgiveness infections; and (4) To emotionally demoralize clergy and church leadership.[14] The net result is that in many congregations, millions of Christian people languish in terrible isolation and loneliness.

One of the greatest theological "giants" of all time was Karl Barth. Barth addresses the Church's need to reach out to people with God's active love and concern. In an interview with Eberhard Busch, a close friend, biographer, and colleague of Barth's named Dr. Busch responds to a question about how he thought Barth would address the difficulties of the modern era. He replies:

> Answer: ...I think he saw the biggest problem as the lonely, isolated men and women. Barth had an interesting dream. Someone said to him, "Would you like to see Hell?" and he said yes. And then he saw a lonely man sitting in the desert. I think that is the danger Barth viewed for modern men and women. He believed that the practice of the Gospel meant to create togetherness among "others." Humans, by nature and the grace of God, are fellow human beings. It is dangerous to be alone. We must learn to live with the "otherness" of others. That is an important point for our time.[15]

Mobilizing Combat Medics

Great care should be given in choosing Christian "combat medics." How the Church cares for its own sends a signal to the world about how or whether we truly love one another. These "combat medics" could be trained, designated, and commissioned by the denomination or local congregation to serve as a roving combat medic among a set jurisdiction of congregations. Any congregation could request their services. These persons would have to be trained in crisis counseling, intercessory prayer, and deliverance ministry. These people would volunteer to go into the thick of conflict situations and exercise spiritual triage until an evacuation was necessary. These "spiritual flight surgeons or combat medics" should have courageous and bold personalities. Their authority to do this kind of ministry would be bestowed by either the particular congregation or preferably by a group of congregations.[16] The goal of military medicine is summarized in the Army's Field Manual 8-10-6. One particular section of the manual is entitled *Supporting the Battle.* It states:

> Medical Commanders must effectively use their resources to treat, evacuate, and, when possible, return to duty (RTD) sick, injured, and wounded soldiers. In the initial phases of battle, the soldiers who are treated and returned to duty provide the tactical commanders with the only source of trained combat replacements. The term *return to duty soldiers* denotes the sick, injured, or wounded soldiers who have been medically treated within the theater and returned to active service.[17]

Like soldiers in military service, Christian "combatants" need to be returned to active duty as soon as possible. Many would be able to do just that if properly triaged and treated. However, there are many believers who are essentially spiritual and emotional "prisoners of war," suffering from what is similar to post traumatic stress disorder.

Prisoners of War

Military POWs never fully recover from the trauma and indignity of being taken captive. The residual effects of being deprived of personal freedom and physically malnourished and tortured never fully heal. Senator John McCain's five and a half years in North Vietnamese prison camps testifies to the inhumanity of the experience. And yet, McCain also witnesses to the fact that God does seek us out even when we are in utter despair. God takes great pleasure in holding out hope to His children.

Once I was thrown into another cell after a long and difficult interrogation. I discovered scratched into one of the cell's walls the creed I believe in God, the father Almighty.' There, standing witness to God's presence in a remote, concealed place, recalled to my faith by a stronger, better man, I felt God's love and care more vividly than I would have felt it had I been safe among a pious congregation in the most magnificent cathedral.[18]

Many of God's people are prisoners of spiritual and emotional wars. Just as McCain was tortured and alone, so, too, are many believers. Just as McCain was severely beaten and mistreated, so too are men, women, boys, and girls who name the Savior's name. One of the imprisoning experiences so many people face is what is called a "father wound." It is caused by traumatic events perpetrated by fathers on their children. I received a significant "father wound" as a result of my father being taken prisoner by the German Army during World War II's "Battle of the Bulge."

He has been a diagnosed sufferer of Post-Traumatic Stress Disorder for nearly sixty years. His trauma scarred my entire family. My mother, sister and I bore the brunt of the anger, irritability, tension, and most of all, emotional disengagement. For my sister and I, Dad's PTSD created a severe "father wound."[19] The effects of secondary traumatization are substantial...

In the Journal of Nervous and Mental Disease an article entitled, "Impact of Post-Traumatic Stress Disorder of World War 2 on the Next Generation", Dr. Robert Rosenheck states: '...the perspective of the children, their father's PTSD could be identified as a distinct and relatively isolated family stressor that had been present throughout their lives.'[20]

The realities of "father wounds" result in wounded children. Millions of people both in and out of the Church suffer from what is called the "wounded child within." These children, who later move into adulthood, always carry residual effects, even if Christ heals them later in life.

J. Pleck in *The Father Wound* says, '...The psychological or physical absence of fathers from their families is one of the great underestimated tragedies of our time.'[21] Research also indicates that there are many adult children who carry through life this 'wounded child within.' A study by Shere Hite in 1981 surveyed 7,239 men with precisely this condition. Accordingly, 'almost no men said they had been or were close to their fathers.'[22]

Battlefield Aid Stations and Combat Stress Control

The Army has determined that when soldiers experience a psychological overload due to combat stress or "battle fatigue," the most successful RTD rates stem from providing soldiers with "expectancy."

Expectancy refers to an overarching clinical attitude that has been recognized since World War I to be essential in restoring soldiers and returning them to duty. The treatment team's collective attitude of expectancy shapes the various physical, psychological, and environmental interventions to bolster the patient's self-confidence as a soldier and discourage self-protective feelings and invalidism (e.g., to reduce the secondary gain wish for medical exemption from further combat.[23]

During both the Korean and Vietnam wars, military doctors treated soldiers suffering from battlefield trauma by the so-called "exhortative" approach.

> ...The soldier is managed more as a soldier and less as a patient. While hospitalized, he is regarded as if his symptoms represent simply a temporary, normal reaction to stress and fatigue. He is encouraged to believe that after a brief period of rest and recuperation and with the psychiatric team's assistance in ventilating his traumatic combat experience, he can and will recover quickly, rejoin his comrades, resume his military job, and regain his self-respect.[24]

Many believers want and need someone to pull them off the front lines for a time to encourage and exhort them in their personal spiritual battle. A familiar expression may accurately describe what many feel. We often say to each other "How goes the battle?" Life is a battle indeed. I believe that all spiritual warriors need a group of like-minded Christians to perform duties—what the Army describes as "Stress Control Teams." There are many stresses associated with combat. In Army Field Manual 8-51 *Combat Stress Control in a Theater of Operations-Change 1*, it says, "In one's own soldiers... control of stress is often the decisive difference between victory and defeat across the operational continuum... Soldiers that are properly focused by training, unit cohesion, and leadership are most likely to have the strength, endurance, and alertness to perform their combat mission."[25]

If battle fatigue can affect soldiers on a physical battleground, spiritual warriors dealing with both earthly and heavenly forces can also experience stresses that weary, frustrate, and utterly discourage them. Pastors are very susceptible to burnout and despair. Many suffer silently from "spiritual battle fatigue." I once made this observation about spiritual combat stress:

> I wonder how many Christian soldiers all across this nation are experiencing "combat stress"? In my pastoral ministry these twenty-five years, I have seen many wonderful

workers for the Lord (both clergy and laypersons) who have been in so many battles they are just plain tired, discouraged, and sad. Andre Gide once said, "Sadness is almost never anything but a form of fatigue." In combat there is a non-clinical description of soldiers who have seen their fair share of battle. They are often aptly described as having a "thousand yard stare". The fight has just gone out of them. Soldiers, who have fought so long and intensely, frequently develop a kind of ambivalent attitude. They become almost callous and insensitive to their own needs and cannot see sometimes how they negatively influence others.[26]

I contend that to perpetuate healing among the thousands of "battle-fatigued" Christian workers in the United States and the world, teams of spiritual "combat stress control teams" are desperately needed. While it is true that many denominations already have mechanisms in place that visit and counsel fellow clergy persons, the effort is more often reactive than proactive in nature. Trained teams of caring laypersons and clergy could be dispatched to provide crisis ministry and preventive care. The Army has four stated goals for dealing with battle-fatigued soldiers: (1) Reassure of normality, (2) Rest (respite from work), (3) Replenish physiologic status, and (4) Restore confidence with activities.[27] These four goals succinctly describe what Christian workers need today.

Satan has masterfully worn many in the Church down to the point where leaders and parishioners alike are afraid of facilitating their own health and vision. Leonardo Boff comments on this state of affairs.

Through the latter centuries, the church has acquired an organizational form with a heavily hierarchical framework and a juridical understanding of relationships among Christians, thus producing mechanical, reified inequalities and inequities. As Yves Congar has written, 'Think of the church as a huge organization, controlled by a hierarchy, with subordinates whose only task is, to keep the rules and follow the practices. Would this be a caricature? Scarcely?'[28]

Throughout this book, I have attempted to demonstrate that while the U.S. Army is far from a perfect institution, its "war-fighting" doctrine has something significant to contribute to the Church. The French military scientist Ardant du Picq tells an interesting tale about four men and a lion. He says, "Four brave men who do not know each other will not dare attack a lion. Four less brave men, but knowing each other well, sure of their reliability and consequently of mutual aid, will attack resolutely." I believe it is time for Christian soldiers—both men and women—to rise up and attack the lion that the Apostle Peter alludes to in his first epistle (I Peter 5:8). I am prepared to make some specific recommendations for the Church's future battle plan.

PART VI. RECOMMENDATIONS FOR THE CHURCH AT LARGE

CHAPTER TEN

UNDERSTANDING THE NATURE OF SPIRITUAL WAR

This book has attempted to highlight various "doctrinal" under-standings of the attitudes and practices of the United States Army. The Army is dramatically changing how it trains, leads, and sustains itself as it plans towards building the so-called Objective Force. War planners are actively fighting the battles of the year 2025.

The Church and individual Christians are also called to "transfor-mation" as they wage spiritual "war." The Apostle Paul reminds us of the importance of transformation in Romans 12:2. He says, "Do not conform any longer to the pattern of this world, but be *transformed* (Italics mine) by the renewing of your mind." (NIV) Believers are not to be content with either their personal spiritual growth or main-taining the status quo of the Church. The un-reached peoples of the earth will not be won to Christ without a radical altering of the Church's strategy and tactics. The Church of Jesus Christ is called by its Lord to grow. Growth implies and even demands change! Just as the United States Army is developing a new "warrior ethos," so too must the Church infuse its members with a new fighting spirit. I recommend that the Church adopt and fashion a different attitude concerning "spiritual combat." The recommendations focus on intelligence, leadership, tactics, training, and caring for its wounded.

Increasing the Church's Intelligence Capabilities

Recommendation 1: In order for denominations, regional judicatories, and local congregations to recognize and assess satanic threats to families, youth, marriages, and other positive societal entities, an Office of Spiritual Intelligence and Threat Analysis must be established. This office would operate best at the regional level. Various churches could pool their most spiritually discerning people to formulate an intelligence estimate similar to what the U.S. Army produces. The intelligence product would provide "actionable" intelligence on Satanic attempts to deceive, divide, and destroy faith-based organizations and their efforts. These "threat" analyses would be refined and updated quarterly or whenever denominational leaders requested new information.

Recommendation 2: I believe that the Church should develop an interactive computer software program to train Church leaders as the Army Military Intelligence Creed says: "to find, know, and never lose the enemy." This program could be called the SIPB (spiritual intelligence preparation of the battlefield). This software could be ideally used at the congregational level to analyze where Satan is likely to attack. The training tool would focus on known tactics of Satan and project community vulnerabilities. The tool would assist Christians in achieving "situational awareness" so that they could effect lasting change in their communities. The program would also be used to devise possible counter-tactics to thwart and nullify demonic activity. In keeping with the Army's IPB process, the training tool would instruct church leaders and other interested persons to (1) define the battlefield environment, (2) describe the battlefield's effects, (3) evaluate the threat, and (4) determine threat courses of action.

What Kind of Leadership Does the Church Really Need?

Recommendation 1: Develop multi-level "leadership academies" patterned after the non-commissioned and commissioned officer's career progression courses. Pastors, "apostles," or denominational executives will select participants. Students will include both lay and clergy persons. Classes will focus on subjects to include: The spiritual warrior ethos, people leading methods and skills, core values, creating and sustaining vision, conflict resolution, intercessory prayer, deliverance ministry, and other locally relevant topics. The POI will draw heavily on vignettes from Church history. Great care will be given to furnish students with an inter-denominational experience that seeks to emphasize a scenario-driven, practical, problem-solving curriculum. The philosophy of these "academies" could be modeled after the Army's Center for Lessons Learned (CALL) at Fort Leavenworth, Kansas. The CALL's mission is to "collect and analyze data from a variety of current and historical sources, including all Army operations and training events, and produces lessons for military commanders, staff and students."[1]

Recommendation 2: I urge individual congregations to explore instruction that concentrates on developing a "spiritual warrior ethos." The core of this training would be to formulate a list of essential "combatives" that define for Christians what mission essential tasks are needed to advance discipleship and evangelism. The Army's Training and Doctrine Command's "Warrior Ethos" statement could be used as a template.

Tactical Lessons in Conducting Spiritual Warfare

Recommendation: It is my view that most Christians have little or no knowledge about the differences between strategy and tactics. I recommend that denominations and individual churches invite Christian instructors of military science or active duty military persons to provide semi-annual symposia on strategy and tactics. These lectures would be purposely interactive with parishioners and concentrate on how the military approaches plans, operations, logistics, and decision-making when confronting an enemy. The goal would be to help people draw parallels in the conduct of their "spiritual combat operations." Insights will be sought from military strategists like Clausewitz, who said, "The strategist must...define an aim for the entire war...In other words, he will draft the plan of the war, and the aim will determine the series of actions intended to achieve it..."[2] Most American believers need to be completely re-educated in the fundamentals of New Testament spiritual warfare. They neither know the "aim" of the Church or the necessary actions to realize the kingdom of God. A study of Army doctrine could help people make spiritual applications.

New Training Paradigms

Recommendation 1: Develop discipleship training standards that are uniform throughout a church judicatory. Establish a program akin to "Initial Entry Training" for new Christians. This "Basic Combat Training School" or "believers' boot camp" would have five phases like the Army. It should last at least twelve weeks. In the beginning, new Christians will be required to undergo rigorous training in spiritual fitness and weapons familiarization (study of Scripture, prayer and inner life disciplines, church history, discovering spiritual gifts, introduction to teams). The goal is to create a dramatic shift from benign discipleship to a posture that leads new Christians into a spiritual warrior mentality. A separate six to eight week "advanced individual training" school would be established to focus more on evangelism, "Stephen's Ministries," and empowering Christians to specialize in areas of service that require a unique calling by God and possibly ordination to full-time ministry.

Recommendation 2: Establish drill sergeant/instructors (DS/DI) schools for congregational junior lay leaders. In the Army, a DS's mission is "to inspire the recruit to be the best soldier he/she can be through knowledge and training."[3] These schools would seek to elevate Christian discipleship training to a highly professional level. The Army's nine Principles of Training (see page 112) will be used as a guide for all training. Junior drill sergeants with less than five years' experience will serve as individual or group coaches and mentors for parishioners. Senior "drill" sergeants who have five to eight years "hands on" experience in congregational ministry will be eligible to become drill instructors (DI). They will be the paramount trainers or advisors for a denomination or church association. I recommend that a judicatory train a sufficient number of DS's so that there is one DS for every one hundred adult Christians. Each week, there will be an established "sergeant's time" not less than two hours in length. DDS's will gather their charges for specialized combative training. An individual congregation will establish this training so that it is interests-based. Core discipleship subjects will be taught while also encouraging congregational creativity and need. The ratio for a senior DI should be one for every three hundred adult Christians. Individual denominations/associations should "commission" them to serve for a minimum of five years. Individual congregations should have the right to accept or reject their placement and should publicly install them in their assigned duties. Each denomination/association will establish a separate Board of Discipleship Standards that will recruit, train, and monitor the ministries of DS's and DI's and constantly refine discipleship training so that it is "battle-focused." This board would function as a kind of Army Training and Doctrine Command.

Caring for the Church's Wounded

Recommendation 1: Establish congregational "combat life-savers." I propose that many Christians and congregations urgently need a more responsive system to identify and "treat" spiritual trauma and injury. To do so, people who especially have the spiritual gifts of wisdom, mercy, knowledge-discernment, and teaching should be trained and deployed as spiritual combat life-savers. I recommend that in an average-sized congregation of one to two hundred members, at least ten percent of the congregation should be trained as combat life-savers. The goal of such a program would be to return the Christian soldier to "active duty" as soon as possible. CLSers would emulate the army's AMEDD to "begin at the place of injury or onset of illness."[4] The training for dispensing what the Army calls "foot-locker" counseling should include topics in basic counseling skills, spiritual healing, deliverance ministry, and referral protocols. CLS training could be conducted by identified Christian psychologists or gifted pastoral counselors. One possible model for such training is what is now being offered by an organization called *Presbyterian-Reformed Ministries International.* (PRMI) They are located at 115 Richardson Boulevard, P.O. Box 429, Black Mountain, North Carolina 28711-0429. This training initiated by PRMI recently trained forty men and women in the United States and the United Kingdom.[5]

Recommendation 2: Establish ten regional spiritual healing training centers in the Northeast, Southeast, Midwest, Northwest, and Southwest areas of the United States. Two centers would be located in each region. Instructors for these programs would be recognized by the Church in healing and deliverance ministry and possess at least ten years in relevant ministry. These teaching centers would be multi-disciplinary in nature and modeled after the Army's medical centers, like Walter Reed Medical Center in Washington, DC. These centers would provide a six-month internship course and a year residency instruction program. Students would be sought from among pastors, hospital chaplains, laypersons, and from Christian doctors, nurses, psychologists, social workers, drug and alcohol counselors, domestic violence counselors, and other selected paraprofessionals. To participate in the training, students would incur a ministry obligation of two years within an approved ministry location. The approving authority would be the person's own denomination or church association.

CONCLUSION

I have attempted to draw an extended comparison between the war-fighting doctrine of the United States Army and its possible theological applications to spiritual warfare. While the Army is far from an ideal institution, it does have something to contribute to the Church. The Army is rediscovering its "warrior ethos." The Church needs to do the same! In essence, the fire of the Holy Spirit needs to be frequently *rekindled* in order for the kingdom of God to be advanced. In 2 Timothy 1:6, the apostle Paul exhorts his protégé with these words: "...I remind you to kindle afresh the gift of God which is in you through the laying on of my hands." (NASV)

The Church's fighting spirit desperately needs to be rekindled. Perhaps this illustration is an apt conclusion for this book.

> The other day I watched a few minutes of a documentary on a group of people, a tribe, if you will, who are nomadic and very simple. They move their camp from place to place as the food supply demands. These people have no idea how to start a fire and they have no need to know, because they carry a live coal, wrapped in green leaves, from campsite to campsite. It's a reminder of the sacredness and fragility of life to stop and consider how they, as a people, have survived over the centuries by the same fire whose eternal coals have been passed from hand to hand and generation to generation.[6]

Just as the Army today is engaged in its Transformation Program so, too, must the Church of Jesus Christ. The Apostle Paul implores Timothy to "rekindle" the gifts God gave him. The Lord of history earnestly desires for the Church to glorify Him by being "firestarters." May the eternal flame of God's Spirit motivate the Church to be as the old hymn suggests—a "Mighty Army." *Soli Deo Gloria.*

Endnotes

Chapter One:

[1]Geoffrey Cowley, "Our Bodies, Our Fears," Newsweek, 24 February 2003, 44.

[2]J.B. Phillips, The New Testament in Modern English (New York: The Macmillan Company, 1960), 353.

[3]Lester Sumrall, The Militant Church: Warfare Strategies for Today's Christians
(Springdale: Whitaker House Images, 1994), Introduction.

[4]The New International Version of the Bible (Nashville: Broadman and Holman Publishers, 1996), 1034.

[5]Sumrall, *Militant,* 8.

[6]Robert M. Coffey, "A Soldier Looks at the Whole Armor of God" (D.Min. Ministry Focus Paper, Fuller Theological Seminary, 1997), 13.

[7]Gregory A. Boyd, *God at War: The Bible and Spiritual Conflict* (Downers Grove: Intervarsity Press, 1997), 171.

[8]Ibid. 184.

[9]Harold W. Nelson, *The Army,* "This We'll Defend", editor (Arlington, VA: The Army Historical Foundation, Hugh Lauter Levin Associates, Inc. 2001), 41.

[10]Ibid., 42.

[11]Field Manual 100-5, *Operations,* Headquarters, Department of the Army (Washington, DC. 1993).

[12]Eric K. Shinseki, "Concepts for the Objective Force", *United States Army White Paper,*
(Washington, DC: Department of the Army, 2000), Foreword, ii.

[13]Eric K. Shinseki and Louis Caldera, "The Army Vision Statement", (Washington, DC: Department of the Army, 2000), 1.

[14]*Giffard's Pocket Study Guide for the US Army E5 and E6 Promotion Boards*, rev. ed. (Altamonte Springs: 1998), 22.

[15]Oath of Enlistment for Military Services, Title 10, United States Code, May 5, 1960, ratified in Congress, October 5, 1962, available from http://www.home.ptd.net/~larrysch/enlistment.htm, accessed 6 April 2004.

[16]Shinseki, *White Paper,* 2.

[17]Peter Paret, *Understanding War: Essays on Clausewitz and the History of Military Power,*
(Princeton: Princeton University Press, 1992), Foreword.

[18]Faoud Ajami, "Islam's Widening Battleground", *U.S. News and World Report,* 28 October, 2002, 28.

[19]Shinseki, *White Paper,* 2.

[20]Associated Press article, "1,000 Troops Launch Search for Terrorist Cells", quoted in *Army Times,* 31 March 2003, 24.

[21]Samuel P. Huntington, *The Clash of Civilizations* (New York: Simon and Schuster, 1996), 249.

[22]R.W. Southern, *Western Views of Islam in the Middle Ages* (Cambridge: Harvard University Press, 1962), 3-4.

[23]Ajami, *Battleground,* 28.

[24]Brian R. Reinwald, "Retaining the Moral Element of War", *Military Review*, (Fort Leavenworth: Combined Arms General Staff School, January/February 1998), 1.

[25]Earl H. Tilford Jr., "The Revolution in Military Affairs: Prospects and Cautions", (Carlisle: Strategic Institute Report, US Army War College 1995), 1.

[26]*Department of Defense Internal News Archive,* from "Transforming the U.S. Military", Introduction, *updated 14 March 2003,* available from http://www.defenselink.mil/specials/transform/intro.html; Internet; accessed 30 April 2003.

[27]John C. Doesburg, Major General, Briefing for US Army officers given at the Edgewood Area of Aberdeen Proving Ground, Maryland, March 2003.

[28]Paul J. Kern, General, Briefing for US Army Chaplains and Chaplain Assistants entitled "Transformations", given in (Orlando, Florida, 25 February 2003).

[29]Shinseki and Caldera, *Vision,* 2.

[30]Kern, *Transformations.*

[31]Shinseki, *White Paper,* 20.

Chapter Two:

[1]Ron Maxwell, producer, *Gods and Generals,* General Thomas "Stonewall" Jackson's comments to a fellow Virginia Military Institute Professor's about the nature of war, (Burbank: Ted Turner Film Properties, 2002).

[2]Will Durant, quoted in the US Army's Chaplain Officer Advanced Course in "The Role of the Chaplain in Mobilization", C-23 Curriculum, (Ft. Monmouth: US Army Chaplain Center and School, 1990-1991), 25.

[3]Everett F. Harrison, Geoffrey W. Bromiley, and Carl F. Henry, editors, *Bakers Dictionary of Theology* (Grand Rapids: Baker Book House, 1960), 236.

[4]Arthur Campbell Ainger, lyricist, *"God Is Working His Purpose Out,"* music composed by Martin Shaw in *Songs of Praise,* 1931.

[5]John Eldredge, *Wild At Heart* (Nashville: Thomas Nelson Publishers, 2001), 141.

[6]Christopher Idle, *Stories of Our Favorite Hymns,* ed., (Grand Rapids: William B. Eerdmans Publishing Company, 1980), 58.

[7]Eldredge, *Wild,* 141.

[8]Harrison, Bromiley and Henry, *Bakers,* 236.

[9]C.S. Lewis, *The Screwtape Letters* (New York: The Macmillan Company, 1943), 9.

[10]Webster's Revised Unabridged Dictionary, 1996, 1998 MICRA, Inc. available from http://www.dictionary.reference.com/search?q=militant; Internet; accessed 18 October 2003.

[11]The Church Militant Forums, "The Church Militant: Keep the Faith, Defend the Church," [journal on-line] available from http://www.the churchmilitant.org/militant.htm; Internet; accessed 18 October 2003.

[12]The Church Militant Forums, "Why Militant?" [journal on-line] available from http://www.the churchmilitant.org/militant.htm; Internet; accessed 18 October 2003.

[13]Walter Wink, *Unmasking the Powers* (Philadelphia: Fortress Press, 1986), 9.

[14]Morton Kelsey, "The Mythology of Evil," *Journal of Religion and Health*, 13 (1974): 16.

[15]Wink, *Unmasking,* 11.

[16]Clinton E. Arnold, *Powers of Darkness* (Downers Grove: InterVarsity Press, 1992), 154.

[17]Thom S. Rainer, *The Bridger Generation* (Nashville, TN: Broadman & Holman Publishers, 1997), 6-8.

[18]"Sociology at Hewett, Post-Modernism: A Definition"?, available from http://www.hewett.norfolk.sch.uk/curric/soc/POSTMODE/post11.htm; Internet; accessed 18 October 2003.

[19]Ibid.

[20]C.S.Lewis, *Screwtape,* 61.

[21] "Post-Modernism: A Definition?"

[22] "The City and the Stars: Post Modernity with Spirit", available from http://www.vanderbilt.edu/AnS/english/eng1289a/citystar.html; Internet; accessed 12 October 2003.

[23]Claus Westermann, *The Old Testament Library: Isaiah 40-66* (Philadelphia: Westminster Press, 1969), 344.

[24]Eldredge, *Wild At Heart,* 209.

[25]Ross P. Rohde, "The Coming Tidal Wave," *A Report Presented to the European Strategy Group,* 2000, [journal on-line], The Gospel and Postmodernism, available from http://www. bmi.net/bauman/ The Gospel and Postmodernism.htm; Internet; accessed 12 October 2003.

[26]Eberhard Busch, "An Interview with Eberhard Busch," *ReNews,* A publication of Presbyterians For Renewal, March 2000, Volume 11, Number 1, Louisville, KY: March 2000, 5.

[27]A.A. Hodge, *Outlines of Theology, chapter 2,* "The Rule of Faith and Practice," 1860, available from http://www. Geocities.com/ reformedchristian/HodgeScriptures.htm; Internet; accessed 19 January 2004.

[28]Thomas C. Oden, *Requiem: A Lament in Three Movement* (Nashville: Abingdon Press, 1995), 46.

[29]Rohde, "The Coming Tidal Wave", 8.

[30]C.F. Keil and F. Delitzsch, *"Ezra, Nehemiah and Esther,"* by C.F. Keil, translated from the German by Sophia Taylor, Biblical Commentary on the Old Testament (Grand Rapids: William B. Eerdmans Company, 1966), 169.

[31]B. Davidson, *The Analytical Hebrew and Chaldee Lexicon* (London: Samuel Bagster and Sons Limited, 1956), DLXXI.

Chapter Three:

[1]United States Army Foreign Counterintelligence Activity "Change of Command," Program, 24 July 2003, Fort George G. Meade, MD.

[2]Army Field Manual 34-130, *Intelligence Preparation of the Battlefield* (Washington, DC:
Headquarters, Department of the Army, 1994), Chapter 1, Introduction, 1.

[3]Ibid.

[4]Matthew Cox, "Long-Range Recon" *Army Times,* October16, 2000, 18.

[5]Ibid.19.

[6]*Army Times,* Newslines, "Recon School Could Be for Battalion Scouts, Too," October 16, 2000, 19.

[7]Army Field Manual: 34-130, 1.

[8]Army Field Manual: 34-130, 2.

[9]Ibid.

[10]Army Field Manual: 34-130, 3.

[11]Vince Crawley and Rick Maze, "How Could It Happen?" *Army Times,* September 24, 2002, 12; 14.

[12]Army Field Manual: 34-130, 4.

[13]Ernest L. Vermont, "The Treatment and Care of Casualties of War: A Comparative Study Between Army Battlefield Medicine

and the Christian Church's Care for Its Own," (D.Min. course paper November 1999), 21.

[14]Charles Kraft, "Deep Level Healing and Deliverance," Doctor of Ministry Course: MG714, (Pasadena, CA: Fuller Theological Seminary, 1999), 2.3-2.4.

[15]Elaine Pagels, *The Origin of Satan* (New York: Vintage Books, 1995) Introduction, xviii.

[16]Ibid. Introduction, xvii

[17]Pagels, xviii and xix.

[18]James Kallas, *Jesus and the Power of Satan* (Philadelphia: Westminster Press, 1968), 151, in Charles Kraft's "Deep Level Healing and Deliverance" MG714 Doctor of Ministry course outline (Pasadena: Fuller Theological Seminary, November 8-19, 1999), 2.13-2.14.

[19]Kraft, MG714 course outline, 2.5

[20]Ibid. 2.6

[21]Adrian Rogers, *The Incredible Power of Kingdom Authority* (Nashville:
Broadman and Holman Publishers, 2002), 69.

[22]Dietrich Bonhoeffer, *The Communion of Saints,* trans. Ronald Gregor Smith, et al. (New York: Harper & Row, 1963) quoted in Dallas M. Roark and Bob E. Patterson, ed., *Dietrich Bonhoeffer* (Waco, TX: Word Books, first printing, 1972), 31.

[23]Charles Kraft, "Deep Level Healing and Deliverance," Doctor of Ministry Course: MG714, (Pasadena, CA: Fuller Theological Seminary, 8-19 November 1999), class notes taken Ernest L. Vermont.

[24]Kraft, MG714, course outline, 2.8

[25]Ibid.

[26]Kraft, outline, 2.9

[27]Sydney H.T. Page, *Powers of Evil* (Grand Rapids: Baker Books, 1995), 88.

[28]Ibid. 87-88.

[29]Page, *Powers,* 137, quoted from P. Pimental, "The Unclean Spirits of St. Mark's Gospel", *Expository Times,* 99 (1988): 173-175.

[30]Page, *Powers,* 138. in Harper, *Spiritual Warfare* (Plainfield, NJ: Logos, 1970), 137-138; E. Murphy, "We Are at War," in *Wrestling with Dark Angels,* ed. C. Peter Wagner and E.D. Pennoyer, (Ventura, CA: Regal, 1990), 57.

[31]Ibid. 141.

[32]Victor H. Ernest, *I Talked With Spirits* (Wheaton, IL: Tyndale House Publishers, Fifth Printing, 1972), 75-76.

[33]C. Peter Wagner and editors of *Christian Life Magazine, Signs and Wonders Today* (Wheaton, IL: Christian Life Magazine, 1982), Introduction.

[34]George Barna, "Christianity Showing No Visible Signs of a Nationwide Revival" (Ventura, CA: The Barna Research Group, 1998), 2, available from http://www.barna.org/PressNoRevival.htm; Internet; accessed Spring 2000.

[35]C.S. Lewis, *Screwtape Letters,* 44-45.

[36]Wagner, *Signs and Wonders for Today,* 11.

[37]James Kallas, *The Satanward View* (Philadelphia: Westminster Press, 1966), 17, quoted in Charles Kraft's "Deep Level Healing and Deliverance" Doctor of Ministry course MG714 outline, (Pasadena: Fuller Theological Seminary, 8-19 November 1999), 2.1.4.

[38]Kallas, *The Satanward View,* 55-56.

[39]Chuck Lowe, *Territorial Spirits and Evangelisation?* (Great Britain: OMF International, 1998), 10.

[40]Lowe, *Territorial Spirits,* 11.

[41]Ibid. 10.

[42]Ibid. 13.

[43]D.E.H. Whiteley, *The Theology of St. Paul* (Philadelphia: Fortress Press, 1972), 25.

[44]William Barclay, *The Letters to the Galatians and Ephesians: The Daily Study Bible Series, Revised Edition* (Philadelphia: Westminster Press, 1976), 182.

[42]Ibid. 13.

[43]D.E.H. Whiteley, *The Theology of St. Paul* (Philadelphia: Fortress Press, 1972), 25.

[44]William Barclay, *The Letters to the Galatians and Ephesians: The Daily Study Bible Series, Revised Edition* (Philadelphia: Westminster Press, 1976), 182.

[45]Walter Wink, *The Powers That Be: Theology for a New Millennium,* (New York: Doubleday, 1998), 24.

[46]Kraft, MG714 outline, 2.33.

[47]Ibid. 2.35.

[48]Kraft, MG714 course outline, 2.36.

[49]Lowe, *Territorial Spirits,* 32.

Chapter Four:

[1]Army Field Manual: 22-100 (Washington, DC: Headquarters, Department of the Army, 1990), 1.

[2]Army Field Manual: 22-103 (Washington, DC: Headquarters, Department of the Army, 1987), 3.

[3]Major General Peter J. Boylan, "Commander's Commandments," *Mountain Views,*
Tenth Mountain Division Commander's Newsletter, 1, Fort Drum, New York, 3 May 1988.

[4]Army Field Manual: 22-103, *Leadership and Command at Senior Levels,* 2.

[5]Ibid. 4.

[6]Nate Allen and Tony Burgess, *Taking the Guidon* (Delaware: Center for Company-Level Leadership, 2001). 57.

[7]Allen and Burgess, *Guidon,* 1.

[8]Christopher Kolenda, co-author and editor, *Leadership: The Warrior's Art* (Carlisle, PA: The Army War College Foundation Press, 2001), 9.

[9]William G. Bainbridge, "First and Getting Firster," Army Magazine, October 1975, briefing presented at Fort Gordon, Georgia entitled,

"Thin Veneer: The Values of the United States Army" by Chaplain (Captain) Dennis Eugene Hysom, 18 January 2002.

[10]General Peter J. Schoomaker, "Arrival Message," available from http://www.army.mil/leaders/csa/messages/1aug03.htm; Internet; accessed 2 December 2003.

[11]Training and Doctrine Command of the United States Army, from a circular entitled: "The Warrior Ethos," Fort Monroe, Virginia, 2002.

[12] Tice, Jim, "Examples in Leadership," Springfield, VA: Army Times Publishing Company, 16.

[13] Atkinson, Rick, "Ike's Dark Days: How an Unlikely Leader Taught an Unprepared Army to Fight," *U.S. News and World Report*, 28 October 2002, 49.

[14]Omar N. Bradley and Clay Blair, *A General's Life* (New York: Simon & Schuster, 1983), 214.

[15]Ibid.

[16]*A General's Life,* 219.

[17]Alan Axelrod, *Patton: On Leadership* (Paramus, NJ: Prentice Hall Press, 1999). Introduction, xv.

[18]Ibid. xxi.

[19] Axelrod, *Patton: On Leadership,* Preface, xxi.

[20]Ibid. xxiii.

[21]Johnathan Paschall, "A Translation of Clausewitz's 'On War' for Austerlitz's Players", available from http://www.geocities.

com/TimesSquare/Battlefield/5955/art.html; Internet; accessed 29 December 1999.

[22]Ibid.

[23]B.H. Liddell Hart, *Strategy,* second revised edition, (New York: The Penguin Group, 1991, 322-23.

[24]Ibid.332.

[25]Hart, *Strategy,* 333.

[26]Ibid.

[27]Hart, *Strategy,* 321.

[28]Army Field Manual: 22-103, *Leadership and Command at Senior Levels,* 84.

[29]Army Field Manual: 101-5, *Staff Organization and Operations* (Washington, DC: Headquarters, Department of the Army, 31 May 1997), 1-1.

[30]Ibid.

[31]*Staff Organization,* 1-2.

[32]Ibid.1-1.

[33]*Staff Organization,* 1-2.

[34]Ibid.

[35]Norman H. Schwarzkopf, *It Doesn't Take a Hero,* written with Peter Petre, New York: Bantam Books, 1992, quoted from *West Point: The First 200 Years,* Guilford, CT: The Globe Pequot Press, 2002, 175.

Chapter Five:

[1]Eric K. Shinseki, "Leadership and Command", Arlington, VA: The Association of the United States Army, 2002, 64.

[2]Bob Briner and Ray Pritchard, *The Leadership Lessons of Jesus* (Nashville: Broadman & Holman Publishers, 1997), 6.
[3]Bill Thrall, Bruce McNicol and Ken McElrath, *The Ascent of a Leader* (San Francisco: Jossey-Bass Publishers 1999), 11.

[4]John W. de Gruchy, editor, *Dietrich Bonhoeffer: Witness to Jesus Christ* (Minneapolis: Fortress Press, 1987), 217.

[5]Ted W. Engstrom, *The Making of a Christian Leader* (Grand Rapids, MI: Zondervan Publishing House, 1976), 38-40.

[6]Army Field Manual 100-61, *Armor-and Mechanized-Based Opposing Force Operational Art* (Washington, DC: Headquarters, Department of the Army, 26 January 1998) 2: 1.

[7]Everett F. Harrison, *A Short Life of Christ* (Grand Rapids, MI: William B. Eerdmans
Publishing Company, 1968), 92.

[8]Inez Smith, "A Team Leader" (Pasadena, CA: *Theology, News and Notes*, Fuller Theological Seminary, June 1997), 19.

[9]C. Peter Wagner, "Apostles and Intercessors" (Colorado Springs, CO: Global Harvest Ministries, available from http://www.global-harvestministries.org; Internet; accessed 27 January 2004).

[10]C. Peter Wagner, "Introduction to the New Apostolic Reformation," available from http: //www.globalharvest.org/index. asp?action=apostolic; Internet; accessed 24 January 2004.

[11]George G. Hunter III, *Church for the Unchurched* (Nashville: Abingdon Press, 1996), 10.

[12]C. Peter Wagner, *Warfare Prayer* (Ventura, CA: Regal Books, 1992) from article entitled: "The Real Battle is Spiritual", available from http://www.globalharvestministries.org; Internet; accessed 27 January 2004.

[13]Ibid.

[14]Wagner, "The Real Battle is Spiritual" 3.

[15]Ibid.

[16]C. Peter Wagner, *Engaging the Enemy* (Ventura, CA: Regal Books, 1991), article entitled: "Spiritual Warfare" available from http://www.globalharvestministries.org; Internet; accessed 27 January 2004.

[17]Chuck D. Pierce, "Apostolic Praying that Unlocks Regions," (Denton, TX: *Global Prayer News*, Volume 1, No.2, April-June 2000) available from http://www.globalharvestministries.org,; Internet; accessed 27 January 2004.

[18]C. Peter Wagner, "Random Notes: Understanding How Apostles Minister in Different Spheres" revised 16 March 2001, available from http://www.globalharvestministries.org; Internet; accessed 12 February 2004.

[19]Ibid.1.

[20]Internet article, "International Coalition of Apostles: Frequently Asked Questions," available from http://www.globalharvestministries.org; Internet; accessed 12 February 2004.

[21]C. Peter Wagner, "Apostles and Intercessors," available from http://www.globalharvestministries.org; Internet; accessed 27 January 2004.

[22]Ibid.

[23]Ibid.

[24]Edward Murphy, "We Are At War," available from http://www. globalharvestministries.org quoted from C. Peter Wagner and F. Douglas Pennoyer, *Wrestling with Dark Angels* (Ventura, CA: Regal Books, 1990) Internet; accessed 27 January 2004, 3.

[25]James Montgomery Boice, *The Minor Prophets: An Expositional Commentary, Volume 1, Hosea-Jonah,* (Grand Rapids, MI: Zondervan Publishing House, 1983), 64.

[26]Peter Pett, "Commentary on Ezekiel" available from http:// www2.enigmasoftwaregroup.com/TMP.html; Internet; accessed 13 February 2004.1

[27]Gerhard Kittel, Gerhard Friedrich, editors, translated by Geoffrey W. Bromiley, *Theological Dictionary of the New Testament,* Volume VII, (Grand Rapids, MI: William B. Eerdmans Publishing Company, 1971), 413.

[28]Ibid. 414-15.

[29]Kittel, *Theological Dictionary,* 415.

[30]William Wilson, *Wilson's Old Testament Word Studies,* Unabridged Edition (McLean, VA: MacDonald Publishing Company, ISBN0-91-7006-27-5), 474.

[31]Chuck Pierce, "Prayer for Massachusetts Ruling on Same Sex Marriage," E-mail message from SandyHeacock@charter.net, USSPN (New England) Regional Coordinator to pna@strategicprayer.net, accessed 12 February 2004, 1.

[32]Chuck Pierce, "Prayer Update from Israel: 12 February 2004," E-mail message from pna@strategicprayer.net, sent 13 February 2004, to ataqchap@cs.com (Ernest L. Vermont)

[33]Richard D. Nelson, *Joshua*, The Old Testament Library (Louisville: Westminster John Knox Press, 1997), 21.

[34]W. Phillip Keller, *Joshua: Man of Fearless Faith* (Waco, TX: Word Books Publisher, 1983), 26.

[35]Nelson, *Joshua,* 22.

[36]Alfred Edersheim, "Israel in Canaan Under Joshua and the Judges," Bible History Old Testament, Volume 3, Chapter Seven, Philologos Religious Online Book, available from http://www.owner-bpr@ philologos.org; Internet; accessed 22 January 2004.

[37]Wagner, "Random Notes", 3.

[38]Ibid. 3-4.

[39]C. Peter Wagner, "Three Types of Personal Intercessors," *Prayer Shield*, (Ventura: Regal Books, 1992) available from http://www. globalharvestministries.org; Internet; accessed 27 January 2004.

[40]Ibid. 12.

[41]Internet article: "Intercession and Spiritual Warfare," available from http://websearch.cs.com/cs/boomframe.jsp?query=global+h arvest+ministries&page=1&offset=0&result_url=redir%3Fsrc%3, Internet, accessed 27 January 2004.

[42]Matthew Henry, *Commentary on the Whole Bible,* dated 1712, available from http://www.apostolic-churches.net/bible/mhc/ MHC26022.HTM, Internet; accessed 15 February 2004.

[43]Robert Louis Wilken, *The Spirit of Early Christian Thought* (New Haven: Yale University Press, 2003), 214.

[44]Ibid. 221.

[45]Aurelius Prudentius Clemens, *Psychomachia,* 14 and 904, quoted in Wilken's *The Spirit of Early Christian Thought,* 229.

Chapter Six:

[1]Kitttel, *Theological Dictionary,* 136-37.

[2]TRADOC Regulation 350-6, *Initial Entry Training Policies and Administration,*
(Fort Monroe, VA: Department of the Army, Training and Doctrine Command, November 30, 1998). 1-4, a-b.

[3]Glen E. Morrell, "What Soldiering Is All About," *ARMY* Magazine, October 1986, 40-42.

[4]Army Field Manual 25-101, *Battle Focused Training* (Washington: Headquarters,
Department of the Army, September 30, 1990), 2-2.

[5]Paul Meredith, electronic mail message "VTCIPR Slides Version3" forwarded from Brigadier General Michael Lenaers, Chief of U.S. Army Ordnance Center and School, Aberdeen Proving Ground, Maryland, 1 February 2004.

[6]Lieutenant General Cavin, "Initial Entry Training for An Army at War," a briefing by the IET Review Task Force on 30 January 2004 at Fort Knox, Kentucky.

[7]Ibid. 3.

[8]Cavin, "Training for an Army at War", 8.

[9]Ibid. 11.

[10]Army Field Manual 25-100, *Training the Force* (Washington: Headquarters,

Department of the Army, 15 November 1988), 2c.

[11]Ibid.

[12]Jim Rice, "Recruiting Blitz Centers on Cash," *Army Times*, 6 December 1999. 8-9.

[13]TRADOC Regulation 350-6, 2-3b.

[14]Sean D. Naylor, "Chief of Staff to Soldiers: You're a Riflemen First," *Army Times*, October 20, 2003. 14.

[15]Ibid.

[16]Naylor, "Rifleman First", 14.

[17]SMA Jack L. Tilley, "NCO Vision" available from http://www.us.army.mil; Internet; accessed September 1, 2003.

[18]William T. Licatovich, "The NCO's March in Army History," *Sergeant's Business:* March-April 1989. 21.

[19]Charles T. Tucker, "NCOs: The Passport to Effective Training," *Engineer*, March 1988, 3.

[20]James Bradley, *Flyboys* (Boston: Little, Brown and Company, 2003), 42-43.

[21]R.W. Zimmerman, "Memorandum for Commanding General at Fort Carson, CO: Retirement After Twenty Years of Service" published in Colonel David Hackworth's *Voice of the Grunt* Newsletter, 26 July 1999, available from http://www.d-n-i.net/fcs/comments/c302.htm; Internet; accessed February 29, 2004.

[22]Mark R. Lewis, "Time to Regenerate: A GenX Response to Dr. Wong's Monograph," November 2000, available from http://www.d-n-i.net/fcs/lewis_gen-x.htm; Internet; accessed February 29, 2004.

[23]Ibid. 3.

[24]Mark R. Lewis, "The Definition of Fodder" in "The Specter of Taylorism is Haunting the E-Ring..or Why Promoting Lieutenants to Captain Quicker is a Dumb Idea," 11 June 2002, available from http://www.d-n-i.net/fcs/comments/c451.htm; Internet; accessed 29 February 2004.

[25]*Army News Service*, 14 May 2002, available from http://www.d-n-i.net/fcs/comments/c451.htm; Internet; accessed February 29, 2004.

[26]Lewis, "Taylorism is Haunting the E-Ring", 5.

[27]Ibid.

[28]Bob Krumm, "Fix the Source of the Leak," available from http://www.d-n-i.net/fcs/comments/c451.htm; Internet; accessed February 29, 2004.

[29]Dick Feagler, "American Honor" in *The Plain Dealer*, Cleveland: Ohio, received from electronic message from Chaplain Arthur Pace at PaceA@usachcs-emh1.army.mil, September 30, 1998 to Ernest L. Vermont at PPPREACHER@aol.com

Chapter Seven:

[1]David Foley, "Warrior Ethos Affects All: Warrior Ethos to Strengthen Bodies, Minds," *The Bayonet*, Fort Benning: Georgia, January 13, 2003, 1.

[2]Warren, Rick, *The Purpose Driven Life* (Grand Rapids: Zondervan Publishing House, 2002), 281-82.

[3]Army Field Manual 25-100, *Training the Force*, Chapter 2.

[4]Ibid.

[5]Cynthia Woolever and Deborah Bruce, *A Field Guide to U.S. Congregations* (Louisville:
Westminster John Knox Press, 2002. 71.

[6]Warren, *Purpose Driven Life*, 282.

[7]Woolever and Bruce, *Field Guide*, 71-2.

[8]The Constitution of the Presbyterian Church USA, *The Book of Order,* Form of Government, G3.0103 (Louisville: Published by Office of the General Assembly, 2003.)

[9]Dom Lorenzo Scupoli, *The Spiritual Combat* (Rockford, IL: Tan Books and Publishers, Inc., 1990), Preface, viii.

[10]Ibid.

[11] David Neff, "The Passion of Mel Gibson," *Christianity Today,* March 2004.34.

[12]Charles Kraft, *Christianity with Power* (Ann Arbor, MI: Servant Publications, 1989.), 124.

[14]Kraft, *Christianity with Power*, 175-6.

[15] James Berardinelli, "Chariots of Fire," Warner Brothers, 1981, film review, 1996, available from, http://www.movie-reviews.colossus.net/movies/c/chariots.html; Internet; accessed March 7, 2004.

[16]Wayne Cordeiro, *Doing Church as a Team* (Ventura: Regal Books, 2001), 45.

[17]Ibid. 44.

[18] John Caroll and Steven Dana, "The Military's Money Men," *American Way*, August 1, 2003, 67.

[19]Ibid.

[20]Cordeiro, *Doing Church as a Team*, 47.

[21]George G. Hunter III, *Church for the Unchurched* (Nashville, TN: Abingdon Press, 1996), 10.

[22]Cordeiro, 48.

[23]Gregg F. Martin, George E. Reed, Ruth Collins, and Cortez K. Dial, "The Road to Mentoring: Paved with Good Intentions," *Parameters,* (Carlisle Barracks, PA: The Army War College, Autumn 2002), 4, available from http://carlisle-www.army.mil/usawc/Parameters/ 02autumn/martin.htm; Internet; accessed March 7, 2004.

[24]Ibid.

[25]Lynn Anderson, "Is Spiritual Mentoring a Biblical Idea?" available from http://www.heartlight.org/hope_990407_mentoring.html; Internet; accessed March 6, 2004.

[26]Ibid.

[27]Martin, Reed, Collins and Dial, "The Road to Mentoring," 11.

[28]Anderson, "Spiritual Mentoring," 2.

[29]Leith Anderson, *A Church for the Twenty-First Century* (Minneapolis: Bethany House Publishers, 1992), 222.

[30]Non-Commissioned Officer's Creed" available from http://www. armystudyguide.com/nco_duties/nco_creed.htm; Internet; accessed March 10, 2004.

[31]Non-Commissioned Officer's Guide, available from http://www. geocities.com/plankmaker_1999/NCO.html; Internet; accessed March 10, 2004.

[32]Hans Wilhelm Hertzberg, *I and II Samuel: A Commentary,* translated by J.S. Bowden,
rev. ed., (Philadelphia: The Westminster Press, 1960), 405.

[33]Neil Eskelin, "Serve Your Sheep," available from jumpstartlist@ neileskelin.com; *Daily Jump Start,* July 16, 2001.

Chapter Eight:

[1]Army Field Manual 8-10-6, *Medical Evacuation in a Theater of Operations* (Washington, DC: Headquarters, Department of the Army, 1991), 1-2.

[2]Ernest L. Vermont, "The Treatment and Care of Casualties of War: A Comparative Study Between Army Battlefield Medicine and the Christian Church's Care for Its Own," (D.Min. course paper, Fuller Theological Seminary, March 2000), 49.

[3]Army Field Manual 8-35, *Evacuation of the Sick and Wounded* (Washington, DC: Headquarters, Department of the Army).

[4]David Eddy, *Triage for Year 2000 Efforts,* American Heritage Dictionary, 1993, available from www.comlinks.com/mag/detria. htm; Internet; accessed March 23, 2000.

[5]Derlet, Robert, "Triage," available from http://www.emedicine. com/emerg/topic670.htm; Internet; accessed March 18, 2004.

[6]Army Field Manual 4-02.4, *Medical Platoon Leader's Handbook* (Washington, DC:
Headquarters, Department of the Army, August 24, 2001), chapter 2-3.

[7]C. Christopher Hook, "The Techno Sapiens Are Coming," *Christianity Today,* January 2004, 40.

[8] "Combat Life-Savers," *The Fort Bragg Post,* 20 November 1996, updated for 2002), available from http://www.geocities.com/Pentagon/Quarters/2116/combatlifesaver.htm; Internet; accessed March 18, 2004.

[9]TRADOC Pamphlet 525-66, "Military Operations Force Operating Procedures,"11-6. FOC-11-05, "Global Casualty Care Management and Evacuation," available from http://www-tradoc.army.mil/tpubs/pams/P525-66.htm; Internet; accessed March 20, 2004. 1.

[10]Ibid.

[11]TRADOC Pamphlet 525-66, "Military Operations," 2.

[12]Ibid.

[13]Army Field Manual 1-113, *Utility and Cargo Helicopter Operations* (Washington: Headquarters,
Department of the Army, September 12, 1997), 6-1.

[14]Ibid.

[15]FM 1-113, 6-3.

[16]John McCain and Mark Salter, *Faith of My Father* (New York: Random House, 1999), 252-54.

[17] "The Ranger Creed," available from http://www.nightstalkers.com/creed/ranger.html; Internet; accessed March 20, 2004.

[18]Joe Light, "Defending 'Leave No Man Behind Policy,'" *The Yale Herald,* Undergraduate Publication of Yale University, 5 April 2002, VOL. XXXIII, NO.10, available from http://www.yaleherald.com/article.php?Article=532; Internet; accessed March 20, 2004.

[19]Ibid.

[20]Light, "No One Left Behind Policy"

[21] "One Nation Under God-Sort of," an editorial from "Where We Stand," *Christianity Today,*
January 2004, 34.

[22]Ibid.

Chapter Nine:

[1]Ernest L. Vermont, "Casualties of War: A Comparative Study, etc.," 8-9.

[2]Rhonda Cornum as told to Peter Copeland, *She Went to War* (Novato, CA: Presidio Press, 1992), 196.

[3]Rod Burton, "Spiritual Pain: A Brief Overview and an Initial Response within the Christian Tradition," *The Journal of Pastoral Care and Counseling,* vol. 57, no.4, Winter 2003, 438.

[4]Milton W. Hay, "Building Spiritual Assessment Tools," *The American Journal of Hospice and Palliative Care,* Sept/Oct 1989, quoted in Rod Burton, "Spiritual Pain: A Brief Overview and an Initial Response Within the Christian Tradition," *The Journal of Pastoral Care and Counseling,* vol. 57, no. 4, 438.

[5]Burton, "Spiritual Pain: An Overview," 440-1.

[6]*Manual for Living Water's Computer Assessment Program,* chapter 6, "Spiritual Injuries," available from http://www.spiritualassessment.com/manual.htm; Internet; accessed March 24, 2004.

[7]Paul W. Pruyser, *The Minister As Diagnostician* (Philadelphia: The Westminster Press, 1976).

[8]Lawrence G. Seidl, *Quality Assurance & Pastoral Care: A Development and Implementation Guide* (St. Louis: The Catholic Health Association of the United States, 1990).

[9]Larry VandeCreek, "A Research Primer for Pastoral Care and Counseling,"
Journal of Pastoral Care Publications, Inc., (1988): 3.

[10]Gary E. Berg, *Living water Computer Assessment Program* 1992, Software is available for purchase from Living Water Software, 1203 7th Avenue North, St. Cloud, MN 56303.

[11]Melba R. Banks and C. Garland Vance, *Multi-level Spiritual Assessment: An Introductory Manual,* provided at the Unit Ministry Team Training, August 23- September 3, 1999 (Asheville, NC: Veterans Administration Medical Center, 1999).

[12]Melba R. Banks and C. Garland Vance, "Spiritual Screen/Spiritual Assessment Level 1," from *Multi-level Spiritual Assessment: An Introductory Manual,* provided at Unit Ministry Team Training, August 23 –September 3, 1999, (Asheville, NC: Veterans Administration Medical Center, 1999).

[13] Neil T. Anderson, *Victory Over Darkness* (Ventura, CA: Regal Books, 1990), 56.

[14]Vermont, "The Treatment and Care of Casualties of War: A Comparative Study," 23.

[15]Eberhard Busch, An interview with Dr. Karl Barth's biographer in *ReNews:* A publication of Presbyterians for Renewal, March 2000, Vol. 11, No. 1., Louisville, KY: March 2000. 3-7.

[16]Vermont, 47.

[17]Field Manual 8-10-6, *Medical Evacuation in a Theater of Operations,*

(Washington, DC: Headquarters, Department of the Army, 1991), 1-2.

[18]McCain and Salter, *Faith of My Fathers,* 252-54.

[19]Vermont, "The Treatment of Casualties of War," 26.

[20]Robert Rosenheck, "Impact of Post Traumatic Stress Disorder of World War II on the Next Generation," *Journal of Nervous and Mental Disease,* vol. 174, no.6, June 1986, 319-27.

[21]J. Pleck, *"The Father Wound,"* in The Center for Research on Women, Wellesley College, MA quoted in *Finding Our Fathers,* by Samuel Osherson (New York: Fawcett Columbine, 1986), 6.

[22]Shere Hite, "The Hite Report on Male Sexuality" (New York: Knopf, 1981), 17.

[23] Franklin D. Jones, L.R. Sparacino, V.L. Wilcox and J.M. Rothberg, eds., *Military Psychiatry: Preparing in Peace for War* (Washington, DC: Office of the Surgeon General, Walter Reed Army Medical Center, 1994), 136.

[24]Ibid.

[25]Army Field Manual 8-51, *Combat Stress Control in a Theater of Operations-Change 1,*
(Washington, DC: Headquarters, Department of the Army, January 30, 1988), 1-1a.

[26]Vermont, "The Treatment of Casualties of War," 31.

[27]FM 8-51, *Combat Stress Control in a Theater of Operations,* 1-6d.

[28]Leonardo Boff, *The Base Communities Reinvent the Church* (Maryknoll, NY: Orbis Books, 1986), 1.

Chapter Ten:

[1]Army Center for Lessons Learned (Fort Leavenworth, Kansas); available from http://www.call.army.mil/mission.htm; Internet; accessed March 31, 2004.

[2]Johnathan Paschall, "A Translation of Clausewitz's 'On War' for Austerlitz's Players," available from http://www.geocities.com/TimesSquare/Battlefield/5955/art.html; Internet; accessed December 29, 1999.

[3]Internet, *Cyber Sarge's*, "U.S. Army Drill Sergeant," available from http://www.cybersarges.tripod/com/drillsgt.html; Internet; accessed April 1, 2004.

[4]Army Field Manual 8-35, *Evacuation of the Sick and Wounded.*

[5]Cindy Strickler, "Advanced Ministry Courses Launched," *Moving with the Spirit,*
Presbyterian-Reformed Renewal Ministries, February 2004, 3.

[6]J. Todd Jenkins, "Firestarter," *Sermonshop*, Internet sermon subscriptions, available from jtoddjenkins@vallnet.com, to sermon-shop@ecunet.org (sermonshop list), September 25, 1998.

WORKS CITED

Allen, Nate and Tony Burgess, *Taking the Guidon,* Delaware: Center for Company-Level Leadership, 2001.

Anderson, Leith, *A Church for the Twenty-First Century,* Minneapolis: Bethany House Publishers, 1992.

Anderson, Neil T., *Victory Over the Darkness,* Ventura, CA: Regal Books, 1990.

_____. 1993. *The Bondage Breaker,* Eugene: OR, Harvest House Publishers.

Arnold, Clinton E., *Powers of Darkness,* Downers Grove, IL: InterVarsity Press, 1992.

Arnold, Eberhard, *Salt and Light* foreword by Jurgen Moltmann, 4th edition, Farmington: PA, 1998.

Avery, J. Stuart, *Nehemiah an Effective Leader,* Chittagong, Bangladesh: Literature Division, Association of Baptists, 1988.

Axelrod, Alan, *Patton on Leadership,* Paramus, NJ: Prentice Hall Press, 1999.

Banks, Melba R. and Garland Vance, Multi-level Spiritual Assessment: An Introductory Manual, Asheville, NC: Veterans Administration Medical Center, 1999.

Barclay, William , *The Letters to the Galatians and Ephesians:* The Daily Study Bible Series, Revised Edition, Philadelphia: Westminster Press, 1976.

Bradley, James, *Flyboys,* Boston: Little, Brown & Company, 2003.

Berkhof, L., *Systematic Theology*, 4th edition, Grand Rapids: MI, 1941.

Blair, Edward P., *The Layman's Bible Commentary: Deuteronomy and Joshua,* Atlanta: John Knox Press, 1977, Fifth Printing.

Boff Leonardo, *The Base Communities Reinvent the Church,* (Maryknoll: NY, Orbis Books, 1986).

Bonhoeffer, Dietrich, *The Communion of Saints,* translation by Ronald Gregor Smith,
et al. New York: Harper & Row, 1963.

Bonn, Keith E., *Army Officer's Guide*, 49th edition, Mechanicsburg, PA: Stackpole
Books, 2002.

Boyd, Gregory A., *God at War: The Bible and Spiritual Conflict*, Downers Grove, IL: 1997.

Bradley, Omar N., and Clay Blair, *A General's Life,* New York: Simon & Schuster, 1983.

Briner, Bob, and Ray Pritchard, *The Leadership Lessons of Jesus,* Nashville: Broadman & Holman Publishers, 1997.

Cordeiro, Wayne, *Doing Church as a Team,* Ventura, CA: Regal Books, 2001.

Cornum, Rhonda and Peter Copeland, *She Went To War,* Novato, CA: Presidio Press, 1992.

Davidson, B., *The Analytical Hebrew and Chaldee Lexicon,* London: Samuel Bagster & Sons Limited, 1956.

De Gruchy, John W., editor, *Dietrich Bonhoeffer: Witness to Jesus Christ,* Minneapolis: Fortress Press, 1987.

De Pree, Max, *Leading Without Power,* Holland, MI: Shepherd Foundation, 1997.

Eldredge John, *Wild at Heart,* Nashville, TN: Thomas Nelson, 2001.

Engstrom, Ted W., *The Making of a Christian Leader,* Grand Rapids, MI: Zondervan Publishing House, 1976.

Ernest, Victor H., *I Talked with Spirits,* Wheaton, IL: Tyndale House Publishers, Fifth Printing, 1972.

Field Manual 1-113, *Utility and Cargo Helicopter Operations,* Washington: Headquarters, Department of the Army, 12 September 1997.

Field Manual 8-10-6, *Medical Evacuation in a Theater of Operations,* Washington, DC: Headquarters, Department of the Army, 1991.

Field Manual 8-35, *Evacuation of the Sick and Wounded,* Washington, DC: Headquarters, Department of the Army, 1983.

Field Manual 8-51, *Combat Stress Control in a Theater of Operations-Change 1,* Washington, DC: Headquarters, Department of the Army, 30 January 1988.

Field Manual 22-100, *Military Leadership,* Washington, DC: Headquarters, Department of the Army, 1990.

Field Manual 22-103, *Leadership and Command at Senior Levels,* Washington, DC: Headquarters, Department of the Army, 1987.

Field Manual 25-100, *Training the Force,* Washington, DC: Headquarters, Department of the Army, 1988.

Field Manual 25-101, *Battle-Focused Training,* Washington, DC: Headquarters, Department of the Army, 1990.

Field Manual 34-130, *Intelligence Preparation of the Battlefield,* Washington, DC: Headquarters, Department of the Army, 1994.

Field Manual 100-5, *Operations,* Washington, DC: Headquarters, Department of the Army, 1993.

Field Manual 100-61, *Armor-and Mechanized-Based Opposing Force Operational Art,* Washington, DC: Headquarters, Department of the Army, 1998.

Field Manual 100-7, *Decisive Force: The Army in Theater Operations,* Washington, DC: Headquarters, Department of the Army, 1995.

Field Manual 101-5, *Staff Organization and Operations,* Washington, DC: Headquarters, Department of the Army, 1997.

Grant, John, James Lynch and Ronald Bailey, W*est Point: The First 200 Years,* Guilford, CT: The Globe Pequot Press, 2002.

Grenz, Stanley J., *A Primer on Postmodernism,* Grand Rapids, MI: William B. Eerdmans Publishing Company, 1996.

Haggard, Ted, *Primary Purpose,* Orlando, FL: Creation House, 1995.

Hands, D. and W. Fehr, *Spiritual Wholeness for Clergy,* Washington, DC: The Alban Institute Inc., 1993.

Harrison, Everett F., *A Short Life of Christ,* Grand Rapids, MI: William B. Eerdmans Publishing Company, 1968.

Harrison, Everett F. and Geoffrey W. Bromiley and Carl F. Henry, (eds.), *Baker's Dictionary of Theology,* Grand Rapids, MI: Baker Book House, 1960.

Hart, B.H. Liddle, *Strategy,* New York, NY: Penguin Books, 1991.

Hertzberg, Hans Wilhelm, *1 and II Samuel: A Commentary,* from the Old Testament Library translated by J.S. Bowden, Philadelphia: The Westminster Press, second edition, 1960.

Hodge, A.A., *Outlines in Theology,* 1860.

Huntington, Samuel P., *The Clash of Civilizations: Remaking of World Order,* New York, NY: Touchstone, 1996.

Idle, Christopher, editor, *Stories of Our Favorite Hymns,* Grand Rapids, MI: William B. Eerdmans Publishing Company, 1980.

Jowett, John Henry, *The Whole Armour of God,* New York: Fleming H. Revell Company, 1916

Kallas, James, *Jesus and the Power of Satan,* Philadelphia: Westminster Press, 1968.

Keil, C.F. and F. Delitzsch, *"Ezra, Nehemiah and Esther"*,by C.F. Keil, translated from German by Sophia Taylor, Biblical Commentary on the Old Testament, Grand Rapids: William B. Eerdmans Company, 1966.

Kolenda, Christopher, *Leadership: The Warrior's Art,* Carlisle, PA: Army War College Foundation Press, 2001.

Kraft, Charles H., *Christianity With Power: Your Worldview and Your Experience of the Supernatural,* foreword by Clark H. Pinnock, Ann Arbor, MI: Servant Publications, 1989.

Lewis, C.S., *The Screwtape Letters,* New York: The Macmillan Company, 1943.

Lowe, Chuck, *Territorial Spirits and Evangelisation?,* Great Britain: OMF International, 1998.

Nelson, Harold W., *The Army,* "This We'll Defend", ed., Arlington, VA: The Army Historical Foundation, Hugh Lauter Levin Associates, Inc., 2001.

Oden, Thomas C., *Requiem: A Lament in Three Movements,* Nashville, TN: Abingdon Press, 1995.

Page, Sydney H.T., *Powers of Evil,* Grand Rapids: Baker Books, 1995.

Pagels, Elaine, *The Origin of Satan,* New York: Vintage Books, 1995.

Paret, Peter, *Understanding War: Essays on Clausewitz and the History of Military Power,*Princeton: Princeton University Press, 1992.

Rainer, Thom, *The Bridger Generation,* Nashville, TN: Broadman & Holman Publishers 1997.

Roark, Dallas M. and Bob E. Patterson, ed., *Dietrich Bonhoeffer,* Waco, TX: Word Books, first printing, 1972.

Ribble, John, editor, *The Hymnbook,* Richmond, VA: Presbyterian Church in the United States, 1955.

Rogers, Adrian, *The Incredible Power of Kingdom Authority,* Nashville: Broadman & Holman Publishers, 2002.

Schaller, Lyle E., *The New Reformation: Tomorrow Arrived Yesterday,* Nashville: Abingdon Press, 1995.

Schwarzkopf, Norman H., *It Doesn't Take a Hero,* New York: Bantam Books, 1992.

Scupoli, Dom, Lorenzo, translation revised by: William Lester and Robert Mohan, *The Spiritual Combat and a Treatise on Peace of Soul,* Rockford, Illinois: Tan Books and Publishers, Inc., 1945.

Shay, Jonathan, *Achilles in Vietnam: Combat Trauma and the Undoing of Character,* New York: Scribner, 1994.

Stedman, Ray C., *Body Life,* Ventura, CA: Regal Books, 1972.

Sumrall, Lester, *The Militant Church: Warfare Strategies for Today's Christians,* Springdale, PA: Whitaker House Images, 1994.

TRADOC Pamphlet 525-66, *Military Operations Force Operating Procedures,* Fort Monroe, VA: Headquarters, United States Training and Doctrine Command, 30 January 2003.

TRADOC Regulation 350-6, *Initial Entry Training (IET) Policies and Administration,* Fort Monroe, VA: Headquarters, United States Army Training and Doctrine Command, 30 November 1998.

Thrall, Bill, Bruce McNichol and Ken McElrath, *The Ascent of a Leader,* San Francisco: Jossey-Bass Publishers, 1999.

Vermont, Ernest L., "The Treatment and Care of Casualties of War: A Comparative Study Between Army Battlefield Medicine and the Christian Church's Care for Its Own", D.Min. course paper, Fuller Theological Seminary, 2000.

Wagner, C. Peter and E.D. Pennoyer, ed. *Wrestling with Dark Angels,* Ventura, CA: Regal Books, 1990.

Warren, Rick, *The Purpose Driven Life*, Grand Rapids: Zondervan Publishing House, 2002.

Westermann, Claus, *The Old Testament Library: Isaiah 40-66,* Philadelphia: Westminster Press, 1969.

Wilken, Robert Louis, *The Spirit of Early Christian Thought,* New Haven: Yale University Press, 2003.

Wink, Walter, *Naming the Powers,* Philadelphia, PA: Fortress Press, 1984.

_____. 1986. *Unmasking the Powers,* Philadelphia, PA: Fortress Press.

_____. *The Powers That Be: Theology for a New Millennium,* New York: Doubleday, 1998.

Woodberry, J. Dudley, *Reflections on Islamic Terrorism,* Pasadena, CA: Fuller Theological Seminary, Fuller Focus, Spring 2002.

Woolever, Cynthia and Deborah Bruce, *A Field Guide to U.S. Congregations*, Louisville: Westminster John Knox Press, 2002.

CPSIA information can be obtained
at www.ICGtesting.com
Printed in the USA
LVHW110204130921
697697LV00003B/90